Management
Level
Psychometric
Assessments

Management Level Psychometric Assessments

Over 400 numerical, verbal and non-verbal practice questions to help you land that senior job

Mike Bryon

KoganPage

LONDON PHILADELPHIA NEW DELHI

Publisher's note

Every possible effort has been made to ensure that the information contained in this book is accurate at the time of going to press, and the publishers and author cannot accept responsibility for any errors or omissions, however caused. No responsibility for loss or damage occasioned to any person acting, or refraining from action, as a result of the material in this publication can be accepted by the editor, the publisher or the author.

First published in Great Britain and the United States in 2012 by Kogan Page Limited

120 Pentonville Road	1518 Walnut Street, Suite 1100	4737/23 Ansari Road
London N1 9JN	Philadelphia PA 19102	Daryaganj
United Kingdom	USA	New Delhi 110002
www.koganpage.com		India

© Mike Bryon, 2012

ISBN   978 0 7494 5691 7
E-ISBN 978 0 7494 6324 3

British Library Cataloguing-in-Publication Data

A CIP record for this book is available from the British Library.

Library of Congress Cataloging-in-Publication Data

Bryon, Mike.
    Management level psychometric assessments : over 400 numerical, verbal and non-verbal practice questions to help you land that senior job / Mike Bryon.
        p. cm.
        ISBN 978-0-7494-5691-7 – ISBN 978-0-7494-6324-3   1. Executives–Psychological testing.   2. Executive ability–Testing.   3. Employment tests.   4. Employee selection.
5. Psychological tests.   I. Title.
    HD38.2.B79 2012
    153.9′4–dc23
                                                                                                        2011036259

Typeset by Graphicraft Ltd, Hong Kong
Printed and bound in India by Replika Press Pvt Ltd

Contents

CHAPTER 1

Psychometric assessments: what are they?

This book gives a succinct account of the purpose and format of leading psychometric assessments, covers the vast majority you are likely to face and provides many hundreds of practice questions with answers and detailed explanations. You will not find another book with so much practice at the managerial level or relevant to so many types of assessment.

A psychometric assessment is not like a blood sample test where you roll up your sleeve and suffer the discomfort of the needle. You have no control over the outcome of a blood test but in a psychometric assessment you should be totally in control. Psychometric assessments lack the certainty associated with the natural sciences. When occupational psychologists talk about the objectivity of their psychometric products they mean that the assessment is, for example, more effective than interview. They do not mean that if you fail an assessment you are inevitability unsuitable for the position or that you would undoubtedly underperform if appointed. Because you have considerable influence over the outcome of a psychometric assessment, you can to an extent determine that outcome. You achieve this through systematic preparation and a winning test technique. It is important that you realize that most candidates who score well in a psychometric assessment have worked hard preparing for it.

Psychometric assessments come in myriad forms; the most widely used assessments are the products of a relatively small number of companies. This book focuses on practice for the psychometric products of the leading international test publishers that are used by the majority of organizational giants in the corporate world. The material, therefore, is relevant to the psychometric assessments you are most likely to face.

One of the leading testing companies is SHL. It operates globally and describes the benefits of using its ability assessments in terms of cost efficiency, objectivity, fairness and effectiveness. It lists the types of ability tests it offers as 'verbal, numerical and inductive reasoning, manual dexterity, numerical computation, visual estimation, mechanical comprehension, technical understanding, fault diagnosis and spatial recognition'. It also has a widely used management and graduate item bank, MGIB. You can find out more at the SHL website (www.shl.com) where you can sit sample tests and receive useful feedback.

Another leading testing company is Watson-Glaser. It produces the most widely used assessment of critical thinking, the Watson-Glaser Critical Thinking Appraisal. This product is described on its website (www.watson-glaser.com) as a tool to identify the candidate with the strongest critical thinking ability and as ideal for use in recruitment, promotion competitions, staff development programmes and succession planning.

From an employer's perspective recruitment is a notoriously difficult business. Bad decisions and bad recruitment practice carry risks of damaging a business and may be open to legal challenge. To maximize the chance of attracting the best candidates many employers advertise their vacancies widely. Once employers have established that you have satisfied the formal requirements for the position they investigate your abilities in a range of competencies relevant to the position. To help scrutinize large numbers of applicants objectively and cost-effectively employers turn to psychometric assessments.

The world of business is increasingly global. Gone are the days when an employer could rely on knowledge of particular universities or schools to ensure the required calibre of candidate. How is an employer to make meaningful comparisons between applicants for their Indian, Chinese, US and European headquarters? The applicants' backgrounds, cultural outlooks and educational profiles will be incredibly diverse. Locations are worldwide so the employer cannot realistically call all applicants in for interview unless they interview locally and are content that the interviewers are equally diverse in their outlook. Test security and confirmation of the candidates' identity are also extremely difficult to manage in such a global situation. Psychometric assessments in this context allow the employer to draw meaningful comparisons. The initial assessments are likely to be online, followed by invigilated assessments conducted at an international assessment consultancy with a worldwide network of assessment centres.

If you face a psychometric assessment it is likely to comprise of more than one assignment. Typically at the management level you will face a battery of assessments. In the case of the SHL GMIB it will comprise:

- verbal critical reasoning;

- numerical critical reasoning; and

- productive thinking.

To complete the battery will involve over one and a half hours of assessment.

You will not always face the same items in a battery of assessments even if they are the product of the same test publisher. The items that make up the battery are customized to the vacancy and the competencies considered essential to it. If for example you apply to train in medicine the battery will comprise assessments on:

- verbal reasoning;

- decision making;

- quantitative reasoning;

- abstract reasoning; and

- non-cognitive analysis.

If you apply for a place on the UK Civil Service accelerated management programme the battery will include assessments on:

- verbal and data interpretation qualifying tests;

- an e-tray exercise;

- written assignment;

- group exercise and presentation; and

- interview.

If you are applying for a technical position in electrical engineering or mechanical engineering then you might expect the battery of assessments to include a fault-diagnosis assessment. If you are applying for jobs in architecture or air traffic control then expect the battery to include a spatial reasoning assessment. An increasingly fashionable assessment is one that involves currency conversion and it features in the battery of assessments used for a variety of positions from banking to commercial pilot.

Not all candidates will be invited to all the assessments that make up a battery. For example in the case of the accelerated management programme for the Civil Service you are only invited to the written assignment, group exercise, interview, etc if you pass the qualifying tests and e-tray exercise. Some qualifications may exempt you from sitting parts of an assessment.

A battery of psychometric assessments is bound to include ability tests in numerical and verbal reasoning. Depending on your graduate course of study or the length of time since you completed formal education these are subjects you may not have studied or for many years, or he may an area in which your training will ensure you excel.

The assessments that you face may be administrated in a number of ways. They may be completed online, with paper and pen, at a computer terminal invigilated by an administrator, or at an assessment centre. However the task is administrated and whatever the particular task, all psychometric assessments are designed so that a score can be awarded and comparisons drawn between candidates. The whole point when used during recruitment is that they allow the administrator to conclude that candidate A did better than B. This is achieved by ensuring that the all candidates at all times experience the same assessment in terms of, for example, the instructions and pre-briefing, resources, time allowed to complete the assessment, and the level of difficulty of the assignment. It is said that the assessment is 'standardized'.

At the management level expect the assessments to last a significant amount of time. To do well in these assessments you have to really 'go for it' and maintain a high level of commitment and concentration for the full duration of the assessments. This makes the assessments a test of your stamina and resolve as well as a test of the competencies being examined.

Once you complete an assessment it is scored to produce a 'raw score', in other words how many points you scored. On its own a raw score means very little. You need to know how your score compares to that of other candidates. For example, if you were to obtain a raw score of 50 per cent and the assignment was a very difficult one in which most candidates obtain low scores, then your score might be rated as good. If, however, most candidates exceed 60 per cent in the assignment then your score of 50 per cent would be considered disappointing. In many cases a raw score is 'norm rated', meaning it is compared to the score of other candidates with education/qualifications backgrounds comparable to your own. Each norm rated score in the various assessments and the competencies they measure will be set out in a matrix to provide a profile of the candidate highlighting his or her strengths and challenges.

Your university course or work history will have prepared you for many things but it may not have prepared you very well for an employer's psychometric assessment. The content may seem to you faulty or arbitrary. You may well question the validity of the whole exercise. You may consider some of the statements made to be factually incorrect. Many very able candidates spend too long on questions, thinking too deeply about them, and their score suffers accordingly. The scientist or engineer may hate the fact that questions are to an extent deliberately ambiguous and that scales and diagrams on computer-administered tests can be distorted. It is common for managers who have 'been there and done it' to feel resentment at being subjected to a psychometric assessment.

All these concerns are entirely valid but they will not help. The test author has designed the question so that there is a correct answer. Yes, the test may well contain controversial or factually incorrect statements and if it does so it is intentional, because you are being tested! Make sure you answer the question, not question the questions. Employers want a flexible worker, the employee who can follow instructions, the person who makes good decisions in a less than perfect world. They are looking for the candidate who can draw the best inference when there are gaps in the information available.

If you want that job and there is a psychometric assignment, then you have to do well in it. So, put aside any intellectual concerns. Accept the fact that you have to work at it in order to do well. You will not get all the questions right – and if you were told the answers, you might disagree with some of them. You just have to accept the situation or withdraw your application and go and do something else. The best-scoring candidates put aside any concerns; they see the assignment as an opportunity to prove to the employer just how good they really are. Make sure that you adopt this winning mindset.

When applying for a job or place on a course, see a psychometric assessment as a competition. If the position is very popular, expect to have to compete against hundreds or even thousands of other applicants. It is important that you realize that you are likely to be facing intense competition and you must achieve a score better than the majority in order to pass through to the next stage in the selection process. You may also have to achieve a well balanced score across a number of sub-tests. Many candidates will have prepared for the assessment, so you should also attend fully prepared or expect to come a rather poor second.

As soon as you are notified that you must complete an assessment find out all you can about it. The most important source will be the official website of the assessment publisher. You should study the information contained there with great care. Be sure that you identify exactly what the assignment comprises. Familiarize yourself with sample questions or a description of the assignment. Study a description of the competencies tested and any examples. Use this information to inform your tactics during the assignment and to identify relevant practice material. For example, if you face an assignment that comprises multiple-choice questions, find out whether incorrect or unanswered questions are penalized. In some tests they are, in others not, and its valuable information because it can guide your tactics in the closing moments of the assignment. If you face an assignment that does not penalize incorrect answers then randomly guessing the answers to any unanswered questions in the last few seconds could help. If the assessment does penalize unanswered or incorrect answers than random guessing won't help and you are better off spending the last moments answering just one more question.

The official site is the most valuable but don't stop there. Continue your research with any links provided with your test notification or on the official website of the assessment publisher. Use a search engine to find more. You will not find a copy of the real assessment but some publishers provide example papers or retired questions for practice. You may well find forums where the assessment is discussed and candidates share advice and describe their experience. There are billions of web pages out there and the information you need is almost certainly part of that enormous quantity of information. The question is, how can you find it? In most cases a basic web search will do. Be sure that you search the titles of each assignment that makes up the assessment as well as the assessment itself and the publisher, and it is always worth having a look at the list of related searches lower down on the page. To undertake a more focused search and reduce the number of miss hits, try putting a + sign between your descriptive words. Then the search engine will only link to pages that have all those words (rather than all the pages that have any of the phrases). Repeat the exercise using different descriptive words. Among other things, Chapter 2 describes how to make best use of the information you collect.

CHAPTER 2

How to stand head and shoulders above the other applicants

This book contains advice and insights as well as practice for the most frequently used management-level psychometric assessments. Practice, and lots of it, will allow you to improve your score in the vast majority of these assessments.

Let's start with an example of how this book will help: the Procter and Gamble (P&G) Global Reasoning Test. You can view a video explaining why the company uses this psychometric assessment and try a practice test at https://pg.sitebase.net/pg_images/taleo/ practicetest.htm. The assessment comprises three papers: numerical reasoning, logic-based reasoning and figure reasoning. If you face the P&G assessment then this book is an ideal source of practice because you will find further practice of each three of these sub-tests in Chapters 3, 4 and 6 respectively. Sources of further practice material are also signposted.

Get assessment wise

No matter the assessment that you face you must get assessment wise – get to understand exactly what the assignment you face involves. You will be astonished at how many people attend not knowing what to expect. The first time they learn the nature of the assignment is when the administrator describes it just before the assignment begins for real. Don't make this mistake: you need to know the nature of the challenge as soon as possible.

The organization to which you have applied should have sent you or directed you to a description of the assignment. If it has not done so, have a look on its website to see if it describes it there or contact the organization and ask it to describe it. Now undertake the web search described in Chapter 1. Be sure to get details on:

- who publishes it;

- how many components it comprises;

- what the title of each is;

- what you have to do at each stage;

- how long you are allowed;

- whether you complete it with pen and paper, at a computer terminal or assessment centre;

- if you face a numeracy test, whether or not a calculator is allowed.

Adopt a winning mindset

When informed as to the nature of the challenge remember you must put aside any feelings of resentment or irritation that you have to sit an assessment: such feelings can be very counterproductive. Try not to wonder about the validity of the process. What you think of it and its predictive value is entirely irrelevant. You need to do well if you are to realize your goal. Do well and an important opportunity will become possible. Focus on only that goal and put all else aside: you really need to let your determination to do well take over your life for a while.

Doing well in a test is not simply a matter of intelligence. It is critical that you realize that to do well you have to try hard too. Over some weeks before the assignment you will need to undertake a programme of review and during the exam you will need to really 'go for it'. Afterwards you should feel mentally fatigued. If you don't then you probably failed to apply yourself sufficiently and may not have fully done yourself justice.

Devise and implement an unbeatable study plan

The high scoring candidates are confident of their abilities. They know what to expect and find few if any surprises. They turn up at the centre or log on looking forward to the opportunity to demonstrate how good they really have become and are able to demonstrate a highly effective technique. To make sure you are such a candidate, begin by preparing a study plan well in advance of the test date.

Step 1. Get clear each stage of the challenge

I will say it again because it is so important: the first thing to do is to make sure that you know exactly what to expect at each stage of the assessment. This should include the exact nature of each task and how long you are allowed. If it is online or administered at a computer screen it is important that you are familiar with the screen icons and format. You want to be able to concentrate on the assignment and not worry about which screen icon you should use.

Step 2. Make an honest assessment of your strengths and weaknesses

To prepare thoroughly for any assessment you should obviously concentrate your efforts to improve in the areas in which you are weakest. You probably already know which part of the assessment you will do least well in were you to take the test tomorrow. But you really need to try to go a step further than this and as objectively as possible assess the extent to which your weaker area(s) will let you down. Only then can you ensure that you spend sufficient time addressing the challenge. You should repeat such a self-evaluation at a number of points in your programme of revision so that you can observe your progress and focus on the area(s) that continue to represent a risk of failure.

Step 3. Plan a programme of practice

Now you need to decide how much time to spend preparing for the challenge. The sooner you start the better, and a little but often is better than occasional long sessions. Take it seriously and avoid the trap of promising yourself that you will start tomorrow. For some candidates tomorrow never comes or comes far too late. A winning plan is likely to involve work over a minimum of two weeks, spending a couple of hours revising three times a week. Some candidates will prepare for a couple of months.

Step 4. Obtain every piece of free material and then buy more

Many candidates facing psychometric assessments cannot find sufficient relevant material on which to practise. Some is available free of charge from your university careers department, as downloads on the internet or in libraries, and you should begin your practice on this free material. Much more is sold either through subscription websites or books and you will almost certainly need to use this additional, purchased, material.

If you also face verbal, numerical or non-verbal reasoning tests you can practise at: www.shl.com and www.psl.co.uk; you have to register. Free practice is also available at www.mypsychometric-tests.com and www.mikebryon.com; at these sites there is no requirement to register. In the Kogan Page testing series you will find, at the advance level:

How to Pass Advance Verbal Reasoning Tests, 2nd edition

How to Pass Advance Numeracy Tests, 2nd edition

How to Pass Graduate Psychometric Tests, 4th edition

Graduate Psychometric Test Workbook, 2nd edition

Advance Numeracy Test Workbook, 2nd edition

How to Pass Diagrammatic Reasoning Tests

How to Pass Data Interpretation Tests, revised edition

On the day

Be sure to attend on the day with the right mental approach. Remember, the candidates who do best are not usually the ones who are fearful or resentful. The winning approach is one in which you attend looking forward to the challenge and the opportunity it represents. You are there to demonstrate your abilities and prove to the organization that you are a suitable candidate. The best candidates approach the assignment with confidence in themselves and their abilities. This should not discourage you. Everyone can develop this approach: the secret is preparation. Turn up fully prepared having spent many hours practising, ready to take advantage of your strengths and having addressed any areas of weakness.

It is obviously really important that you listen carefully to the instructions provided. Appreciate the fact that you may well be feeling nervous and this may affect your concentration, so make yourself focus on what is being said. Much of the information will be a repeat of the test description available on the official website, so read and reread this before the day of the test. Pay particular attention to instructions on how long you have to complete the assignment and be sure you are familiar with the demands of each part of the assignment.

Keep track of the time and manage it so that you complete the assignment. You must keep going right up to the end. Aim to get right the balance between speed and accuracy. In some assignments you are not expected to be able to complete everything in the time allowed, in others most successful candidates do succeed to complete the assignment. It is important that you establish this information from the official website or other sources suggested earlier.

In many instances it is better that you risk getting some question wrong but attempt every question rather than double check each answer and be told to stop before you have finished because you have run out of time. Practice can really help develop this skill.

If you hit a difficult section or lose track of what you wanted to say don't lose heart. Everyone gets some questions wrong and no one submits a perfect assignment. Keep going at all costs: you might go on to excel.

Guessing can pay

If you face a psychometric assessment that comprises multiple-choice questions and you do not know the answer to a particular question, you have little alternative but to guess. In a multiple-choice test with five suggested answers, guessing can offer a 20 per cent chance of getting it right. But you can improve on this if you look at the suggested answers and can rule some out as wrong. This 'educated guessing' can reduce the number of suggested answers and increase your chances of guessing correctly. So always look at the suggested answers to see if you can rule some out as definitely wrong and improve your chances of guessing right. Guessing plays an important part in many candidates' test-taking strategy, especially in the later part of each sub-test when time may be running out.

Educated guessing plays an important role in the closing part of an assignment that penalizes unanswered questions.

If you suffer a disability

If your completion of an assessment could be adversely affected by a disability then speak to the organization to which you are applying and seek its advice on how your requirements can best be accommodated. Provide full details of your condition and be clear on the special arrangements you require. You may be allowed extra time or a test reader or someone to record your answers. Braille or large text versions may be made available.

It is reasonable to expect that your requirements are given proper consideration and where possible are accommodated. Evidence of your condition may be required. Be sure to raise your needs at an early stage so that the organizers have time to accommodate them and you have sufficient time to obtain any formal proof of your condition that they may require.

What to do if you fail

If you are reading this having failed a management psychometric assessment and this has prevented you from realizing a career goal, take heart. It is entirely normal for candidates to fail the more popular assignments on the first or even their first few attempts. It certainly does not mean that you do not have the ability to do the job or course in question. However, it does mean that you need to improve on your performance in the assignments used to recruit to that position.

Failure will not mean that the company will not welcome a future application from you. Should you be successful at a later stage, once you are employed you will be judged by your performance in the job not your past assessments so it will not impinge on your future career prospects within the organization.

It is likely that over half the candidates who sit a psychometric assignment will fail. If this happens to you then ask the organization to provide you with feedback on your score and identify the parts that you had problems with. Recall and note down the nature of the assignment. Be honest with yourself and try to assess what it is that you need to do to pass the next time.

I know candidates who repeatedly failed and it was only when they set about a major programme of revision that they went on to pass. Others simply needed to get more used to the assignment and working under time pressure in an exam-type situation. Remember it is not uncommon for accomplished applicants to fail because they think too long or too deeply about the assignment or question its validity. Their work or study does not prepare them well for something in which they must act quickly and take some risks in the given time.

If you fail, plan a programme of revision and improvement straight away and be sure to concentrate on what you are least good at. Seek out sufficient practice material and get down to some seriously hard work. Apply again as soon as you are able and this time attend fully prepared and confident in your abilities.

It will take courage and determination to try again and to keep working to improve yourself until you pass. But these are qualities of which you can be proud. With the right approach you will address your personal challenges and go on to pass. You will then be able to look back on what you can regard as a significant achievement.

May I take this opportunity to wish you every success in the psychometric assessment that you face.

CHAPTER 3

Numerical assessments

I recently obtained an MSc in Banking and I am currently in London where I am looking for a job in the banking sector.
I have difficulties in obtaining the satisfactory results. I believe my main problem is the speed.

(A reader's query)

Smart working is essential if you are to do well, and tailoring your technique to the demands of the assessment is a sign of working smart. The first thing to do is research the assessments that you face and seek to establish the winning technique. Some numerical assessments demand a lightning-fast approach. For example the Citigroup online numerical test requires a quick, 'no time for second thoughts' approach and the time limit is also tough in the numerical test used by Deloitte. Not all numerical assessments require a breakneck performance and some reward a more considered careful working style. The quantitative papers in the GMAT (the assessment you must pass to get into many top business schools) and the UK Civil Servant Faststream allow sufficient time for a relatively considered, thoughtful approach. The same is true for the RUST advanced numerical reasoning appraisal and the McKinsey Problem Solving Test. These assessments still require a determined, hard-thinking approach but if you rush through them it can count against you because you may find you have time to spare and have unnecessarily risked making mistakes because you failed to take a moment to reflect sufficiently on the questions and suggested answers.

When you face a numerical assessment in which time is tight you must roll up your sleeves, put finer considerations aside and simply go for it and get the job done. This may involve the risk of getting some answers wrong but it is better than being told to stop when you have not answered a significant number of the questions. For some candidates it will require reviewing the basics and honing their command of the key competency assumed in these assessments. Some otherwise very accomplished candidates must undertake a major review of their mathematics competencies prior to taking an assessment at the graduate and management level. They may have to let numerical practice take over their life for a while, especially where competition for vacancies is fierce. If you want to be up there with the best then the hard work will need to start well in advance of the assessment itself. The practice below will certainly help and for many will be sufficient. Some will need more material and they can find it in the following Kogan Page Testing titles:

How to Pass Advanced Numeracy Tests, 2nd edition

The Advanced Numeracy Test Workbook, 2nd edition

How to Pass Data Interpretation Tests, revised edition

Numeracy Test Workbook, 2nd edition

Be aware that in some batteries of assessments one paper may reward speed and another may allow sufficient time for most candidates to double-check their work. You may also be expected to complete some assessments without a calculator or you may find that the online calculator is rudimentary and lacks functions that you take for granted. For example Deutsche Bank is currently using a numerical assessment in which a calculator is not allowed. So remember, do your research. You can find out a great deal from the websites of the publisher of the assessment and by participating in job search and career forums such as www.tomcat4.prospects.ac.uk and the jobs and careers forum at www.thestudentroom.co.uk.

An unavoidable feature of every winning approach is good old-fashioned hard work. Those who succeed are usually those with the greatest tenacity both during the assessment and the time leading up to it. It is no coincidence or surprise that the candidates who are most likely to excel in a quantitative assessment have a background in engineering, maths or science. If you belong to this group then be sure to press home your advantage and attend willing to work very hard during the assessment.

Get off to a flying start

Getting off to a flying start is important in all assessments. These days most numerical assessments are computer-administered and how you start in these assessments can be very important.

Below are a series of short assessments that review key numerical competencies examined by many leading numerical assessments. Treat them as a series of practice starts and use them to perfect a really good start in any numerical assessment. A little practice, often, is best and even the really busy candidate can find 10 minutes without distraction to complete one of these exercises. They will prove especially useful if you have not received graduate-level quantitative training. Note that this material is easier than most manager assessments. This is intentional to give you the opportunity to build proficiency; harder material follows.

You must take time to become entirely familiar with the way in which a computer-based numerical assessment is administered onscreen. When you are invited to take the assessment be sure to follow any links provided where you can read a description of the exercise or become familiar with the screen icons. Otherwise visit the website of the assessment publisher where there is likely to be a description or practice pages. Pay attention to how to use the onscreen calculator if one is provided. Be aware that diagrams on the computer screen can be misleading, especially in the case of geometric shapes, tables and graphs, as the screen can distort the image, the scale or both. Take note of what is said and avoid drawing unnecessary assumptions about the appearance of a diagram, table or graph on the screen. For example, if a shape is described as a cube but on the screen the sides do not all seem quite equal, ignore it and treat the shape as a cube. Equally, if a table or graph says that quality x is the largest but on the screen it looks like quality y is the same or in fact bigger, then take no notice and treat quantity x as the largest.

In all numerical assessment assume that every question counts (in fact some may not because they are being trialled, but you can't tell which these are). Try especially hard to get the first question right, then the first five questions, then all the rest! The opening questions in a computer-administered test may be especially significant, and this is another good reason you should practise getting off to a good start, because these tests are sometimes computer-adaptive. This means that the first question will be of the level that the 'average' candidate should get right, the next question will be a little harder and so on. But, and this is important, in a computer-adaptive test you have to get the question right before the program presents you with the harder questions. Keep getting the questions right and you will soon be following along branches of questions that score you in upper percentiles. Whatever you do, try to avoid a bad start. A bad start is something you should work hard to avoid in any test but especially in a computer-adaptive test. Get the first few questions wrong and the computer-adaptive test will present you with easier questions and you will struggle to get back to the level expected for a good pass. This adaptive process continues through the test, so keep trying to get as many questions as possible right to maximize your chance of being awarded a winning score. Guessing can pay. If you do not know the answer you have little alternative but to guess. Always look at the suggested answers to see if you can rule any out as definitely wrong. If you can then you will improve your chances of guessing right.

Use these practice start questions to get down to some really serious score-improving practice and be sure of the very best start in your real assessment. Read each carefully, calculate your answer and then take a moment to read the question again. When you are sure about your answer 'submit it' and move on to the next question, Adopt and practise this 'no going back' approach – it will give the practice a more realistic feel and is an approach used by many high scoring candidates.

Get the most out of this practice by setting yourself the personal challenge of trying to beat your last score or if you got them all right, match your last score each time. You will need to try hard and take the challenge seriously. That way you will create a realistic assessment feel. If you keep getting one sort of question wrong then focus your practice on that type of question until you improve. Then return to these assessments. Keep practising until you consistently get all the questions right. Achieve this and you can take strength from the fact that you are likely to make a very good start in the assessment that you face. The only thing left to do is to keep up that rate of success through to the end!

You will find hundreds more 'quick practice' questions in the intermediate level Kogan Page titles:

Numeracy Test Workbook, 2nd edition

Ultimate Psychometric Tests, 2nd edition

Some of the questions below are short answer (you enter your answer in the box provided) and others are multiple choice. The first section deals with percentages, the next the increasing common task of currency conversion. The last few practice starts review the principles of geometry (important, for example, in the GMAT assessment you must pass to get a place in a top business school) and are presented in the style of data sufficiency questions. These are becoming widespread with tests such as the RUST advanced numerical reasoning appraisal, which comprises comparison of quantities and sufficiency of information tasks. Obviously skip some of these practice starts if you are already very proficient in these tasks. Even if the assessment that you face does not include questions likes these, they are essential skills and skills you must command if you are to triumph in most numerical assessments. Be sure you attend an assessment confident, fast and accurate in these essential operations.

Enter your answer in the answer box and when you have rechecked you choice move on to the next question. Each comprises 10 questions. Do not use a calculator. Even if the assessment you face allows you to use a calculator you should still do these assessments without one because then you will attend able to do these calculations in your head. You will save time and be more likely to recognize a mistake than if you make one using an unfamiliar calculator.

Quantitative reasoning

Practice start 1

Profit and loss as a percentage of the buying or cost price

In this section calculate the profit or loss as a percentage of the buying or cost price. *Tip:* to find the percentage profit, divide the amount of profit by the buying price and multiply the answer by 100. To find the percentage loss, divide the loss by the buying price and multiply the answer by 100.

Time allowed 10 minutes, do not use a calculator.

Worked example (profit)
If the buying price of an item is £10 and the selling price £12 then what Is the percentage profit?

Answer: 20% profit
Explanation: 12 – 10 = £2 profit, 2 ÷ 10 = 0.2 × 100 = 20

Worked example (loss)
What is the percentage loss if the buying price of an item is £10 and the selling price is £9?

Answer: 10% loss
Explanation: 10 – 9 = £1 loss, 1 ÷ 10 = 0.1 × 100 = 10

1   What is the percentage profit or loss if the buying price is £40 and the selling price is 32?

   A. 20% loss
   B. 20% profit
   C. 25% loss
   D. 25% profit

                                        Answer [A]

2   What is the percentage profit or loss if the buying price is $0.50 and the selling price is $0.80?

A. 55% profit

B. 55% loss

C. 60% profit

D. 60% loss

Answer   C

3   What is the percentage profit or loss if the buying price is £4 and the selling price is £5?

A. 25% loss

B. 25% profit

C. 20% loss

D. 20% profit

Answer   B

4   What is the percentage profit or loss if the buying price is £8 and the selling price is £7?

A. 12% loss

B. 12% profit

C. 12.5% loss

D. 12.5% profit

Answer   C

5   What is the percentage profit or loss if the buying price is £290 and the selling price is £237.78?

A. 18% loss

B. 18% profit

C. 20% loss

D. 20% profit

Answer   A

6 What is the percentage profit or loss if the buying price is £82 and the selling price is £63.14?

A. 20% profit

B. 21% profit

C. 22% loss

D. 23% loss

Answer D

7 What is the percentage profit or loss if the buying price is £20 and the selling price is £25?

A. 24% profit

B. 25% profit

C. 26% loss

D. 27% loss

Answer B

8 What is the percentage profit or loss if the buying price is £370 and the selling price is £358.90?

A. 4% profit

B. 4% loss

C. 3% profit

D. 3% loss

Answer D

9 What is the percentage profit or loss if the buying price is £500 and the selling price is £660?

A. 32% profit

B. 31% loss

C. 30% profit

D. 29% loss

Answer A

10 What is the percentage profit or loss if the buying price is £12 and the selling price is £2.40?

A. 75% loss

B. 75% profit

C. 80% loss

D. 80% profit

Answer C

End of assessment.

Currency conversions

Practice start 2

For a job as a pilot with Cathay Pacific Airlines in Hong Kong – for some people a dream job – you complete a computer-based numeracy test that consists of 33 questions, time-limited to 30 minutes. Pencil and paper are allowed but no calculator. No one seems to make it through the whole exam in the time allowed. Use the following to three practice start exercises to review the fundamentals of currency conversion. These examples are easier than the Cathay Pacific questions but they are important competencies underlying this and other assessments.

Time allowed 10 minutes, do not use a calculator.

Q1   If EC$1 = T$1.5, how many T$ = EC$50?

Answer [75]

Q2   If EC$1 = T$1.75, how many T$ = EC$30?

Answer [ ]

Q3   If EC$1 = T$1.4, how many T$ = EC$80?

Answer [ ]

Q4   If EC$1 = T$0.9, how many T$ = EC$25?

Answer [ ]

Q5   If EC$1 = T$0.15, how many T$ = EC$250?

Answer [ ]

Q6   If EC$1 = T$4, how many EC$ = T$20?

Answer [ ]

Q7   If EC$1 = T$2.5, how many EC$ = T$40?

Answer [ ]

Q8   If EC$1 = T$1.25, how many EC$ = T$2.5?

Answer [ ]

Q9   If EC$1 = T$1.75, how many EC$ = T$7?

Answer [ ]

Q10 If EC$1 = T$1.5, how many EC$ = T$60?

Answer [ ]

End of assessment.

Practice start 3

Time allowed 10 minutes, do not use a calculator.

Q1 If HC$1 = AU$2.5, how many HC$ = AU$20?

Answer [   ]

Q2 If HC$1 = AU$1.8, how many HC$ = AU$9?

Answer [   ]

Q3 If HC$1 = AU$4.5, how many HC$ = AU$18?

Answer [   ]

Q4 If HC$1 = AU$1.6, how many HC$ = AU$8?

Answer [   ]

Q5 If HC$1 = AU$1.1, how many HC$ = AU$55?

Answer [   ]

Q6 If EC$2.5 = T$5, how many EC$ = T$10?

Answer [   ]

Q7 If EC$1.5 = T$6, how many EC$ = T$1?

Answer [   ]

Q8 If EC$1 = T$3.2, how many EC$ = T$48?

Answer [   ]

Q9 If EC$2 = T$8, how many EC$ = T$26?

Answer [   ]

Q10 If EC$2 = T$6, how many EC$ = T$24?

Answer [   ]

End of assessment.

Practice start 4

Time allowed 10 minutes, do not use a calculator.

Q1   If EC$3 = T$3.6, how many EC$ = T$6?

Answer

Q2   If EC$2 = T$2.5, how many EC$ = T$15?

Answer

Q3   If EC$9.5 = T$1, how many EC$ = T$114?

Answer

Q4   If EC$2 = T$3.5, how many EC$ = T$7?

Answer

Q5   If EC$3 = T$6, how many EC$ = T$22?

Answer

Q6   If EC$5 = T$15, how many EC$ = T$18?

Answer

Q7   If EC$3 = T$2.25, how many EC$ = T$3?

Answer

Q8   If EC$4 = T$2, how many EC$ = T$9?

Answer

Q9   If EC$3 = T$6.6, how many EC$ = T$11?

Answer

Q10 If EC$4 = T$1.4, how many EC$ = T$100?

Answer

End of assessment.

Data sufficiency

Practice start 5

The style of these questions is widely described as 'data sufficiency'. You must decide if the question can be answered or confirm the given answer is correct. Two types of data sufficiency question are reviewed here. In one you are provided with a regular mathematical or problem-solving question followed by two pieces of information; you must decide how much of the provided information is the minimum needed to answer it. There are five possible responses: that it is possible to answer with statement 1 alone and not 2; with statement 2 alone and not 1; both 1 and 2 are needed, 1 or 2 alone are sufficient, or the question can't be answered with the information provided. The other type comprises a mathematical statement and you must say if it is true, false or it is impossible to say if the answer is true or false. You do not have to waste time undertaking the calculation or at least the full calculation.

These practice questions review fundamentals of maths. Many but not all review elementary geometry. Some (typically US) graduate and management assessments assume a familiarity with geometry. If you face such an assessment then review this area of mathematics, which you may have not studied since when you were in compulsory education.

Time allowed 20 minutes to complete the 10 questions.

Q1   Are all the angles of a triangle equal?

(1) One internal angle is 60° and the sum of the other to two equal 120°.

(2) It is an equilateral triangle.

A. 1 alone, not 2 alone

B. 2 alone, not 1 alone

C. 1 and 2 together

D. 1 alone or 2 alone

E. 1 and 2 together are not sufficient

Answer _____

Q2 $y^2 - y - 2 = 0$ therefore y is negative.

True

False

Cannot tell

Answer _____

Q3   Is the quadrilateral a square?

(1) All angles equal 90°.

(2) The diagonals divide the shape into four identical triangles.

A. 1 alone, not 2 alone

B. 2 alone, not 1 alone

C. 1 and 2 together

D. 1 alone or 2 alone

E. 1 and 2 together are not sufficient

Answer _____

Q4 64 is both a squared and a cubed number.

True

False

Cannot tell

Answer

Q5 What is the area of an isosceles triangle?

(1) With a base 10m long

(2) With two equal sides 13m in length

A. 1 alone, not 2 alone

B. 2 alone, not 1 alone

C. 1 and 2 together

D. 1 alone or 2 alone

E. 1 and 2 together are not sufficient

Answer

Q6 The sum of all numbers from 20 to 48 is 952.

True

False

Cannot tell

Answer

Q7 Is the triangle right-angled?

(1) A line drawn from the vertical angle to meet the base divides it at the midpoint.

(2) The length of the sides is a multiple of 5, 15, 13.

A. 1 alone, not 2 alone

B. 2 alone, not 1 alone

C. 1 and 2 together

D. 1 alone or 2 alone

E. 1 and 2 together are not sufficient

Answer

Q8 If two 6-sided dice are thrown the probability of the sum of the two faces totalling 5 is 1/9.

True

False

Cannot tell

Answer [   ]

Q9 Can a polygon be divided into three triangles?

(1) It is a pentagon

(2) It has five sides

A. 1 alone, not 2 alone

B. 2 alone, not 1 alone

C. 1 and 2 together

D. 1 alone or 2 alone

E. 1 and 2 together are not sufficient

Answer [   ]

Q10 Confirm that the highest payout is $126,000 more than the lowest payout in a lottery syndicate that wins $399,000 and is split in the ratio 7:3:9.

True

False

Cannot confirm

Answer [   ]

End of assessment.

Practice start 6

Time allowed 20 minutes.

Q1 Is n divisible by 8 with no remainder?

(1) n + 1 is divisible by 8 with integer result.

(2) n + 16 is divisible by 8 with integer result.

A. 1 alone, not 2 alone

B. 2 alone, not 1 alone

C. 1 and 2 together

D. 1 alone or 2 alone

E. 1 and 2 together are not sufficient

Answer [   ]

Q2 A triangle with a base of 5cm has an area smaller than a square with sides of 3cm.

True

False

Cannot tell

Answer [   ]

Q3 A bar of soap costs $1; how much would a similar bar cost?

(1) 2 similar bars have dimensions ¾ of the original.

(2) 3 original bars weigh a total of 18oz.

A. 1 alone, not 2 alone

B. 2 alone, not 1 alone

C. 1 and 2 together

D. 1 alone or 2 alone

E. 1 and 2 together are not sufficient

Answer [   ]

Q4 A parallelogram has diagonals that bisect each other.

True

False

Cannot tell   *Answer* [   ]

Q5 If a ball bearing is dropped into a straight-sided beaker of water 3cm deep how much does the water in the beaker rise?

(1) The radius of the base of the beaker is 7cm.

(2) The radius of the ball bearing is 5mm.

A. 1 alone, not 2 alone

B. 2 alone, not 1 alone

C. 1 and 2 together

D. 1 alone or 2 alone

E. 1 and 2 together are not sufficient

Answer [   ]

Q6 If each side of a square is increased by 30% the area occupied by the square would increase by 69%.

True

False

Cannot tell   *Answer* [   ]

Q7 How far up the wall does the ladder reach?

(1) The wall is vertical.

(2) The angle between the ladder and the wall is 80°.

A. 1 alone, not 2 alone

B. 2 alone, not 1 alone

C. 1 and 2 together

D. 1 alone or 2 alone

E. 1 and 2 together are not sufficient

Answer [   ]

Q8 The size of each interior angle in a pentagon can be known if one angle is 100° and four are equal.

True

False

Cannot tell

Answer [   ]

Q9 What is the value of x?

(1) x/y = 4.

(2) xy = 4.

A. 1 alone, not 2 alone

B. 2 alone, not 1 alone

C. 1 and 2 together

D. 1 alone or 2 alone

E. 1 and 2 together are not sufficient

Answer [   ]

Q10 Two shapes are similar if all pairs of corresponding sides are the same?

True

False

Cannot tell

Answer [   ]

End of assessment.

Practice start 7

Time allowed 20 minutes.

Q1 Can you find the diameter of the circle?

(1) A straight line through the circle is twice its radius.

(2) The circumference can be found with the formula π d (take π to = 3.14).

A. 1 alone, not 2 alone

B. 2 alone, not 1 alone

C. 1 and 2 together

D. 1 alone or 2 alone

E. 1 and 2 together are not sufficient

Answer [   ]

Q2 Confirm that the percentage of numbers between 1 and 50 that end in either a 2 or an 8 is 10%.

True

False

Cannot confirm

Answer [   ]

Q3 Is the quadilateral a square?

(1) It has two pairs of parallel lines.

(2) Its interior angles add up to 360°.

PP.   1 alone, not 2 alone

QQ.   2 alone, not 1 alone

RR.   1 and 2 together

SS.   1 alone or 2 alone

TT.   1 and 2 together are not sufficient

Answer [   ]

Q4 Confirm that 1,500 women who graduate will *not* set up their own business if 15% of the whole sample of graduates starts their own business.

True

False

Cannot confirm

Answer [ ]

Q5 Are two shapes congruent?

(1) The angles of one shape are equal to the corresponding angles of the other.

(2) All pairs of corresponding sides are the same size.

A. 1 alone, not 2 alone

B. 2 alone, not 1 alone

C. 1 and 2 together

D. 1 alone or 2 alone

E. 1 and 2 together are not sufficient

Answer [ ]

Q6 The first number in a series of 3 consecutive numbers with the sum of 57 has a total of 5 factors.

True

False

Cannot confirm

Answer [ ]

Q7 How many sides does a regular polygon have?

(1) The total sides of all the interior and exterior angles = 1800°.

(2) The sum of its exterior angles = 360°.

A. 1 alone, not 2 alone

B. 2 alone, not 1 alone

C. 1 and 2 together

D. 1 alone or 2 alone

E. 1 and 2 together are not sufficient

Answer _____

Q8 Confirm that the probability of drawing two queens consecutively from a pack of 52 cards is 1/221 if the first card is not replaced and then the second card is drawn (assume 4 queens at the start).

True

False

Cannot confirm

Answer _____

Q9 What is the surface area of a cone?

(1) Its length (L) = 7cm and the base is 6cm wide.

(2) The cone has a height of 4cm and the base a radius of 3cm.

A. 1 alone, not 2 alone

B. 2 alone, not 1 alone

C. 1 and 2 together

D. 1 alone or 2 alone

E. 1 and 2 together are not sufficient

Answer _____

Q10 Confirm the sum of all the numbers from 50 to 70 is 1,200.

True

False

Cannot confirm

Answer _____

End of assessment.

Data interpretation

This section will help you prepare for business scenario problem-solving questions of the McKPST type used by the consultancy firm McKinsey to assess all non-MBA graduates. (You are not allowed a calculator in the McKPST.) If you Google 'mckinsey problem solving test' you will find very useful material and free practice papers (see for example www.mckinsey.com).

This section will also help you prepare for the ABLE Financial Appraisal Exercise; for information on ABLE visit www.graduate. abnamro.com. This psychometric tool assesses a candidate's financial and analytical skills, comprehension of financial language and ability to discover data relevant to financial decisions. Be prepared for your verbal comprehension skills (in a financial context) as well as your numerical skills to be tested by ABLE. (If you are concerned about your comprehension of financial language, the *Advanced Numeracy Test Workbook*, 2nd edition, published by Kogan Page, is full of material that will be of help.)

It will help you prepare for an SHL assessment. The data handling is fairly involved and requires you to extract information from multiple data sets (eg charts, profit and loss accounts) and then to work through up to four calculations to reach the answer, combining relevant data from the respective data sets.

Please note that these questions serve primarily as an aid to learning and lead you through the key competencies examined in real tests of data interpretation. The mathematician or engineer may find much of the material too easy. This is because it is intended for all candidates and not just the numerically accomplished. Setting the level of these questions is a necessary compromise and while the level will be right for some candidates I will not have got it right for others. However, it includes questions at the level you can expect in a real psychometric assessment of your data interpretation skills and some hard questions so that you can get used to the idea that you may not get all the questions right in a real assessment. Remember not to use a calculator and if you wish to undertake these assessments against the clock then allow yourself one minute 30 seconds a question.

You will find further useful practice in the *Advanced Numeracy Test Workbook*, 2nd edition.

DATA SET

Cash flow 1 for small company in 2001:

Jan	Feb	Mar	Apr	May	Jun	Jul	Aug	Sep	Oct	Nov	Dec

Expenditure (in $):

Salaries

0	0	0	0	0	0	600	800	1000	1200	1400	1600

Professional fees

800	800	800	800	900	900	800	800	800	800	800	800

Q1 Does the percentage increase in salaries between September and October remain the same, decrease, or increase compared to August–September's increase?

A. Decrease

B. Increase

C. Remain the same

D. Not possible to say

Answer A

Q2 Calculate the National Insurance payment that the company will have to sustain in 2001, given that NI is 5% of salaries.

A. $310

B. $320

C. $330

D. $340

Answer C

DATA SET

Mare supermarkets

Mare is a supermarket chain that has enjoyed many years of uninterrupted revenue growth and high levels of profitability (over the period shown, an average 20% profit margin has been realized on the value of total sales). In 2009, however, a major supermarket chain with a reputation for low prices opened a series of stores in direct competition with each of Mare's outlets. This discovery greatly alarmed the management team at Mare especially given the fact that in a recent survey Mare's customers quoted value for money as the most important factor in deciding where they shop.

Value of total sales revenue

2003	2004	2005	2006	2007	2008
$29.5	$30.4	$31.3	$32.2	$33.2	$34.2

Market research in 2003 found that each of Mare's six supermarket outlets is located in residential areas with an average population of 135,000. Each outlet has 5,400 customers a day. In 2008 the most profitable lines were groceries and processed foods. Research into Mare's competitor showed that it routinely priced goods at 12% below Mare's prices.

Q3 On an average day in 2003 what percentage of the population in which a Mare outlet is located could have been expected to visit the store?

A. 5%

B. 4%

C. 3%

D. Cannot tell

Answer   B

Q4 Which of the following actions would least assist Mare's management team in meeting the threat?

A. An across the board cut of 2.5% in the price of all products.

B. The introduction of a very competitively priced range of everyday essential products.

C. The introduction of a membership scheme that rewarded customer loyalty with very low priced special offers.

D. Offering a series of 'added value' services not offered by the competitor such as free home delivery, longer store opening hours and online shopping.

Answer   D

Q5 How much more profit did Mare show in 2008 compared with 2003?

A. $910,000

B. $920,000

C. $930,000

D. $940,000

Answer

Q6   One member of the management team was concerned that groceries and processed food prices should not be cut in case it undermined customers' perception of quality. Which of the following strategies would have allowed Mare to introduce lower prices while avoiding the suggestion that savings had been made by reducing quality? (Note that more than one of the suggested answers is correct.)

A. Adopt a pricing policy where Mare lowers all its prices but maintains a small premium over the prices of its competitor for all its groceries and processed foods lines.

B. Offer tasting opportunities in the stores so that customers can decide for themselves if quality has been compromised.

C. Introduce a money-back guarantee if a customer is not entirely happy with the quality of their purchase.

D. Cut prices only of the grocery and processed food products that the competitor does not also sell while maintaining the higher price for lines that both stores sell.

Answer   B C

Q7   Mare's management team responded to the threat by cutting all 2009 prices by 9% and forecast that this cut would mean that revenue in 2009 would be 10% lower than in 2008. Much to their surprise, however, the price cut stimulated higher sales volumes and the result was that sales revenue for 2009 ended up only 3% down rather than the 10% forecast. How much better was the actual sales revenue for 2009 over the forecast for that year?

A. 3.42m

B. 2.89m

C. 2.394m

D. 1.026m

Answer   C

DATA SET

Increase in receipts from corporation tax (all sums are $billions):

Receipts	From banking and finance	From all other sectors
2007	5.4	3.6
2008		3.654
2009		3.69
2010	4.24	3.76

Q8   What percentage of all corporate tax receipts in 2007 was derived from banking and finance?

A. 62%

B. 60%

C. 58%

D. 56%

Answer   [ ]

Q9   In 2010 as a % of total receipts how much greater were receipts from banking and finance than all other sectors?

A. 3%

B. 4%

C. 5%

D. 6%

Answer   [D]

Q10 Which is the best estimate of how much greater the % increase between 2007/8 and 2008/9 was for all other sectors?

A. 0.33%

B. 0.5%

C. 0.75%

D. 1%

Answer   [D]

DATA SET

Manufacturing cost of 80 refrigeration units:

Direct material	not stated
Direct labour	not stated
Production overheads	not stated
Total factory cost of 80 units	$2170.56
Recommended selling price to retailers per unit	$91.20

Q11 If the manufacturer were to sell 80 units at a discount of 15% of the recommended selling price, what would be the percentage profit or loss?

A. 55%

B. 60%

C. 65%

D. 70%

Answer   C

DATA SET

On a day in October the ounce prices of gold, silver and platinum were:

Gold US$800
Silver US$40
Platinum US$1,200

Q12 If an investor wanted to exchange on that day in October an ounce of platinum for an ounce of gold and take the balance in silver, how many ounces of silver would he receive?

A. 9

B. 10

C. 11

D. 12

Answer   B

Q13 On that October day a hoard of silver and gold coins is worth US$3,400 and contains 25 ounces of silver. How many ounces of gold does the hoard contain?

A. 6

B. 5

C. 4

D. 3

Answer

DATA SET

Doing Very Nicely Inc:

Group turnover	$2.7bn
Pre-tax profit	$349m
Share price	$13.50
Earnings per share	$0.45

Q14 Calculate the share price/earnings ratio for Doing Very Nicely Inc.

A. 45:1

B. 40:1

C. 30:1

D. 25:1

Answer   C

DATA SET

Information technology national ranking index:

Nation	Ranked position 2012	Ranked position 2011
Singapore	1	+1
United States	2	(–1)
South Korea	4	(–1)
Canada	6	+2
Mexico	8	(–2)
China	41	+9
France	20	(–3)

Q15 France in 2011 was ranked 23rd (23 – 3 = 20).

    A. True

    B. False

    C. Cannot tell

                      Answer   A

Q16 In 2011 Mexico occupied Canada's position.

    A. True

    B. False

    C. Cannot tell

                      Answer   C

Q17 Singapore has returned to the top of the index.

    A. True

    B. False

    C. Can not tell

                      Answer   B

DATA SET

Share	Market price/per share ($)	Earnings per ordinary share ($)
Ultimate	8.4	0.60
South	7.2	0.45
World	2.25	0.25
Standard	7.15	0.56

Q18 Which of the following shares is the most 'expensive' in terms of its price/earnings ratio?

A. Ultimate

B. South

C. World

D. Standard

Answer   B

DATA SET

I'm Good plc:

Group turnover	$1.3bn
Pre-tax profit	$523m
Share price	$30
Earnings per share	$1.2

Q19 Calculate the share price/earnings ratio for I'm Good plc.

    A. 25:1

    B. 26:1

    C. 27:1

    D. 28:1

Answer   A

DATA SET

The PMI

PMI stands for 'purchasing manager's index' and is widely used as an indicator of the state of health of leading economies' manufacturing sectors. The monthly index is based on these indicators: employment, environment, supplier delivery, production inventory levels and new orders. A respondent is asked to indicate for each of these issues whether that month is better than, the same as or worse than the previous month.

A PMI of more than 50 is taken as an indicator of strong expansion in the manufacturing sector while a score of below 50 indicates contraction and a score of 50 means no change from the previous month. An index higher than 52 over time is take to represent expansion (the more it is over 52 the stronger the expansion). A PMI that remains below 48 is taken as an indicator of recession. If in a month the swing is large, this is taken as an indicator of the strength of either the expansion or contraction.

PMI over a continuous 36-month period:

month	1	2	3	4	5	6	7	8	9	10	11	12
Y1	43	42	41	41	41	42	43	43	43	46	47	48
Y2	43	45	45	46	48	50	50	50	53	52	54	53
Y3	51	52	54	56	51	50	48	47	47	45	43	42

Q20 Which period would be interpreted most favourably by the markets?

A. Y2, months 8 and 9

B. Y1, months 9 and 10

C. Y3, months 3 and 4

D. Y2, months 5 and 6

Answer [   ]

Q21 How much greater is the mean than the mode for the period Y2 months 3–6 inclusive?

A. 0.8

B. 1.8

C. 2.0

D. 2.8

Answer [   ]

Q22 Which suggested answer best reflects the interquartile range for the PMI over the 36-month period?

A. 41–56

B. 49

C. 48, 52

D. 45–52

Answer [   ]

DATA SET

Commodity price index % change:

	One month	*One year*
All items	+0.38	+4.81
Food	+0.69	+6.36
Services	+0.13	+5.89

Q23 What is the mean monthly change in price for food?

    A. +0.69

    B. +0.61

    C. +0.58

    D. +0.53

Answer

DATA SET

Profit and loss account for Big Bikes (first six months):

Month	M1	M2	M3	M4	M5	M6	H1
Sales (in $)	0	20000	0	40000	0	50000	110000
Costs of sales	0	13600	0	27200	0	33900	74700

Operating costs (in $)

Administration costs	25800	27100	27100	28400	28400	29100	165900
Other expenditure	12500	33800	25200	17200	16500	18700	123900

Q24 Which month yields the greatest gross profit?

A. 6

B. 5

C. 4

D. 3

Answer 6 A

Q25 Which month has the greatest operating costs?

A. 1

B. 2

C. 3

D. 4

Answer B

DATA SET

Sales of three items:

Total sales	*225 units*
Item 1	27 units
Item 2	135 units

Q26 What % of sales does the third item account for?

   A. 25%

   B. 26%

   C. 28%

   D. 30%

Answer   C

DATA SET

Royal Tea

Market research findings relating to Royal Tea:

Market A
Competitor brands are winning
  Royal Tea's market share
Price-sensitive market
Customers base buy decision
  almost entirely on price
Brand is sold at modest premium
  over competitors

Market B
Market-leading brand

Sold at a premium price
High level of customer loyalty
  (low level of brand switching)
Customers perceive higher price to
  imply higher quality

Value of total sales of Royal Tea (000):

	2002	2004	2006	2008
Market A	$120	$121	$115	$119
Market B	$20	$19	$18	$19

Q27 What is the value of sales in market B for the period
2002–2006?

A. 390.0

B. 39.0

C. 3.9

D. Cannot tell

Answer   D

Q28 Sales in market A in 2007 were at the mean value of the figures for that market in 2006 and 2008. What was the value of sales that year?

A. 116

B. 117

C. 118

D. Cannot tell

Answer [   ]

Q29 Market B can be described as the most niche market because it is the most lucrative subset of the whole?

A. True

B. False

C. Cannot tell

Answer [   ]

Q30 Which measure would *not* help sales in market B?

A. Lower the price

B. Increase marketing

C. Increase the price by a small percentage

D. Cannot tell

Answer [   ]

Q31 Sales for market B were 15% better in 2007 than 2006. What was the value of sales in that market that year?

A. 19.2

B. 19.9

C. 20.7

D. 21.2

Answer [C   ]

Q32 The sales manager explains that the principal strategy to improve sales over recent years has relied on trade represent- atives. To break with the past, which of the following strategies would you recommend to most likely result in an increase in sales in market A while maintaining the price premium?

A. A push strategy

B. Mass advertising promoting the quality of the product

C. Trade press advertising promoting the quality of the product

D. Mass advertising promoting discount coupons

Answer [   ]

Q33 Sales for both markets totalled a disappointing 119 for 2003 and were earned at the same ratio between markets A and B as in 2003. What was the value of market A that year?

A. 102

B. 103

C. 104

D. 105

Answer [   ]

Q34 By how much did sale values fall in market A and B combined between 2004 and 2006?

A. $17,000

B. $7,000

C. $70,000

D. Cannot tell

Answer [D   ]

Q35 If the value of sales for the two markets combined in 2002 represented 5% of global sales for the Royal Tea brand, what was the value of global sales that year?

A. 2,800

B. 2,300

C. 1,800

D. Cannot tell

Answer [   ]

Q36 In market B the average pack of Royal Tea costs $3.80 and at this price the profit per pack is $0.57. Use this data to calculate how much profit was made in market B in 2002.

A. $2,250

B. $2,750

C. $3,000

D. Cannot tell

Answer [*C*   ]

DATA SET

Manufacturing costs for producing 50 television (TV) sets:

Direct materials	£1,500
Direct labour	£750.0
Factory overheads	£3,500
Total factory cost for 50 TV sets	£5,750
Recommended selling price to retailers per set	£128.8

TV sets sold (million):

Year:	2007	2008	2009
	2.7	2.1	1.2

TV viewing habits (hours spent watching TV in a typical week):

Hrs of viewing	No of viewers
20–24	200
25–29	600
30–34	900
35–39	400

Q37 70% of sales in 2007 and 2009 occurred in the EU and US territories; how many more TV sets were sold into these territories in 2007 than in 2009?

A. 1.03m

B. 1.04m

C. 1.05m

D. Cannot tell

Answer | C |

Q38 Use the figures provided to calculate the total factory cost of producing all the TV sets sold in 2008.

A. 241.5m

B. 240m

C. 235.5m

D. Cannot tell

Answer   *A*

Q39 From the table, calculate the absorption cost of each TV set (absorption cost = total factory cost divided by the number of units produced).

A. £115

B. £116

C. £117

D. £118

Answer   *A*

Q40 Calculate the marginal cost of each TV set (marginal cost = direct material and labour cost divided by number of units produced).

A. £46

B. £45

C. £44

D. £43

Answer   *B*

Q41 What is the percentage profit/loss made on each TV set (use absorption cost in this calculation)?

A. 9%

B. 10%

C. 11%

D. 12%

Answer   *D*

Q42 By how much would total profits increase or fall in relation to the profit made on 50 sets sold at the recommended selling price if 50 more sets were produced (at marginal cost) without incurring any increase in factory overheads and all 100 sets were sold to retailers at £89?

A. Increase by 200

B. Increase by 205

C. Increase by 210

D. Increase by 215

Answer

Q43 What would the percentage profit be on 50 sets priced at absorption cost and 50 at marginal cost, if all 100 sets were sold at £91.20?

A. 14%

B. 15%

C. 16%

D. 17%

Answer

Q44 What fraction of viewers watch TV for the average number of hours or more?

A. 11/21

B. 13/21

C. 14/21

D. Cannot tell

Answer

DATA SET

Morning Tea

Market research findings relating to Morning Tea

Market A

Competitor brands are winning
 Morning Tea's market share

Price-sensitive market

Customers base buy decision
 almost entirely on price

Brand is sold at modest premium
 over competitors

Market B

Market-leading brand

Sold at a premium price

High level of customer loyalty
 (low level of brand switching)

Customers perceive higher price to
 imply higher quality

Value of total sales of Morning Tea (000):

	2005	*2006*	*2007*	*2008*
Market A	$120	$120.304	$119	$119.696
Market B	$20	$19	$18	$19

Units of Morning Tea sold into market A:

Year	*(000)*
2004	58.3
2005	80
2006	82.4
2007	92.7
2008	93.9

Q45 If Morning Tea were to be sold without a premium over competitor products, what would you expect to be the effect on the level of sales in the two markets?

A. Markets A and B would both increase

B. Sales in market A would increase but B would remain the same

C. Sales in market B would decrease but A would show no change

D. Sales in market B would decrease but market A would increase

Answer [   ]

Q46 How many times bigger is market A than market B?

A. x6.5

B. x6.4

C. x6.3

D. x6.2

Answer [   ]

Q47 You were in a meeting with the finance director and he questioned one of the market research findings. Which one do you think he was referring to?

A. That Morning Tea is sold at a premium in market B

B. Competitor brands are winning Morning Tea's market share in market A

C. That market A is price sensitive.

D. That market B is the market leading brand

E. Cannot tell

Answer [   ]

Q48 In market A for how much less did a unit of Morning Tea sell in 2006 compared with 2005?

A. 2 cents

B. 3 cents

C. 4 cents

D. 5 cents

Answer [   ]

Q49 In 2004 the unit value in market B was 30% that of market A. The same year market A's unit price was 3% lower than its 2005 price. What was the value of sales for the two markets in 2004?

A. $110,274.45

B. $111,274.45

C. $112,274.45

D. $113,274.45

Answer [   ]

DATA SET

Cash flow for Bella in 2011; income (in $):

	Jan	Feb	Mar	Apr	May	Jun	Jul	Aug	Sep	Oct	Nov	Dec	Total
1. Opening	0												0
2. Director's	?												?
3. Other	80000												80000
4. Sales	0	1000	2000	2500	3000	4000	3500	3000	?	4500	6000	7000	41000
Total	90000	1000	2000	2500	3000	4000	3500	3000	?	4500	6000	7000	131000

Q50 How much must the director lend the firm, in order for the total income to be £131,000?

A. $7,000

B. $8,000

C. $9,000

D. $10,000

Answer

DATA SET

Share	Market price/per share ($)	Earnings per ordinary share ($)
Fast	9.8	1.4
Sure	5.4	0.9
Right	8.8	2.2
Best	9	1.8

Q51 If everything else is taken to be equal, which share would you recommend to buy based on the price/earnings ratio?

A. Fast

B. Sure

C. Right

D. Best

Answer [   ]

DATA SET

The base-weighted price index is calculated as follows:

$$\frac{\text{Total cost of base-year quantities at current prices}}{\text{Total cost of base-year quantities at base-year prices}}$$

The price (in pence) for the three commodities being consumed in Country X is represented below, together with the amounts of each consumed. 2011 is the current year and 2010 is the base year.

Year	2010		2011	
	price	*quantity*	*price*	*quantity*
	(p0)	(q0)	(pn)	(qn)
Fish (per pound)	240	20	290	25
Potatoes (per pound)	w	x	y	z
Milk (per pint)	27	200	29	190

Q52 Which of the following are needed in order to calculate the base-weighted price index? (Your answer will include more than one of the suggested answers.)

A. w

B. x

C. y

D. z

Answer [   ]

CHAPTER 4

Verbal assessments

This chapter provides loads of practice questions for the most common sorts of advanced verbal assessments including advice on presentations, written assignments and group exercises.

At some stage in your career you are certain to face a verbal reasoning psychometric assessment. It can involve multiple-choice tests of your work-related verbal abilities; tests of your command of English usage; reading comprehension; written assignments; group discussions or presentations. If you are a graduate or applicant to managerial positions or postgraduate courses you are very likely to face a psychometric test of your advanced verbal skills.

Beyond the first stages of a recruitment process your qualifications count for little. Once employers have established that you have satisfied the formal requirements for the position they then turn to investigate your abilities in a range of other competencies relevant to the position; these are bound to including your verbal reasoning skills.

There are certain things you will have to get used to with verbal reasoning tests. There is a distinct lack of certainty in comparison to numerical questions. In maths there is a right answer and little room for argument. But verbal tests are less definite because they are often concerned with judgement, inference and context.

It is not usual for candidates to feel that the answer they selected is at least as correct as the given answer. If you ever find yourself in this situation the likelihood is that you have to work some more to bring your judgement more into line with the question setters. Verbal reasoning assessments are only indicators of potential and you (the subject) have considerable influence over the outcome.

Verbal reasoning assessments come in many forms and at different stages of your career and at different stages of a recruitment process. To begin with make sure your application and/or CV are error free. They are a sort of verbal assessment. Many organizations will reject your application out of hand if they find errors: you would not believe the number of candidates rejected at this early stage for this easily avoidable reason.

Verbal reasoning assignments are always being changed and novel assessments trialled and introduced. A few years ago, for example, they were most likely to include questions that asked you to identify synonyms and antonyms or tested your spelling or command of the rules of English grammar. These styles of question are still used, especially at the intermediate level, but contemporary tests at the advance level are more likely to comprise a passage of information and a series of related questions to which you have to answer true, false or cannot tell. Another increasingly common verbal assignment involves decision analysis. You are provided with a set of codes and their meanings and must identify the 'best fit' from a list of suggestions.

You may be assigned a task and asked to study a briefing file of documents, sometimes against a tight time constraint. You may then have to write a response to a task assigned to you. The in-tray exercise is an example of this type of assignment and usually involves, for example, details of a fictitious but comparable organizational structure, policy documents and reports on performance, e-mails from imaginary colleagues, letters from suppliers and customers. You will be expected to read the background information and then make recommendations to your line manager in response to a series of e-mail-style questions. See Chapter 5 for practice for 'situational awareness' questions in which you are presented with a workplace situation and must indicate which approach is most appropriate.

The group exercise or role-play

The topic or topics you are assigned to discuss vary from company to company, but you will find that group exercises are fundamentally similar in that you will be one of number of candidates and you must engage in consensual discussion.

1. Preparation time

Group exercises start with time to prepare. During the preparation time, list points that you feel are very important and make sure that these come up in the discussion. Don't worry if someone raises one of your points before you got the chance to make it; just contribute to its discussion and help develop the issue. Sometimes you will get to meet the other candidates before the exercise starts; if you do, use this time to get to know them. You most likely will be told not to appoint a chairperson. Aim to play to your strengths. If maths is your thing, use the data they give you to work out some relevant figures (you should include figures even if maths is not you thing). It is vital to listen to others. They will be looking to see if your input helps to move the group forward, and whether you help the group to achieve its objectives.

In some cases you are given a great deal of briefing information – almost more than you can read in the time allowed. If this is the case, review the material quickly and keep your notes very brief. You might decide on an assessment tool to help in the handling of the briefing papers, such as SWOT and PEST (strengths, weaknesses, opportunities, threats; and political, economic, social, technological). Another commonly used tool is the spider diagram, which is great for speed, recall and the emphasis of connections. Prepare these tools and think through these strategies before the day.

If you find that you do not have enough time to read all the background material, decide what you want to say and use the time you have to make absolutely sure you have sufficient evidence to back up what you plan to say.

You are likely to be briefed as a group, and these are the people with whom you will discuss the topics. If it is appropriate and the opportunity presents itself, take the trouble to get to know some of the group. This will really help with any nervousness you may suffer. You will find it so much easier to have a constructive conversation with someone you have talked to before.

2. The discussion

The discussion will be observed and notes taken by the assessors; it may even be recorded on video. Push all this out of your mind as much as possible and keep your thoughts on the group, its objective and the discussion.

Try to avoid taking notes during the exercise. If you really must take notes, keep them extremely brief – just one-word notes – as you really do not want the invigilator to notice that you are 'looking down'. You want them to notice lots of eye contact and nods in agreement and to conclude that you can listen and have understood the significance of the contribution of others by modifying your position to take account of their contribution.

If you can, and the opportunity presents itself, speak first so that you make the first impression and demonstrate drive. Don't worry if your position is entirely different from everyone else's; you are being assessed on how you make your case, not what case you are making. So set out to make as good a case as you can for the view that you are representing, but also point out its weaknesses. Make sure you are enthusiastic even when discussing what might seem very mundane issues.

Be assertive in getting your points across, but be very careful not to stray into language that could be taken as aggressive. Listen as well as talk. Do make lots of eye contact and do nod in agreement, but don't shake your head or demonstrate your disagreement through body language. Consider making explicit reference to how you have modified your case to take into account the contributions of others. Do this by, for example, offering supportive summaries of others' contributions and then adding a further relevant point of your own.

Recognize the talents and merit in other people's contribution without diminishing your own. Use 'us' and 'we' to emphasize the collective purpose. Suggest criteria to clarify and evaluate the project. Help draw out quieter candidates by creating the space for them to speak. Do this by helping to ensure that everyone has a say. Show decisiveness and leadership qualities but avoid adopting the role of chair.

Don't take criticism personally. Don't start or get sucked into an argument, but in the unlikely event that one occurs, try to help make peace between the parties. This is important and a point on which many otherwise good candidates fail, so be sure to show empathy and go out of your way to resolve tension or disputes that arise between the other parties.

Be prepared to adopt the suggestions of others over your own, as this will be taken as an indication of your willingness to support another's project, of flexibility and of a talent in the building of relationships. Be constructive in your contributions and be supportive of others in your group. Keep your contributions to the point and spell out the relevance if you refer to something not immediately significant to the issue under discussion. Remember to back up all your points with facts and figures from the background material.

3. Self-evaluation of your performance

It is common for you to be asked to complete a self-assessment of your performance at an assessment centre. Take this exercise seriously as it is often scored and counts towards your overall mark. If appropriate, comment on both what you learnt from it and on how you might improve, were you to attend the event or take the exercise again. Keep your self-criticism positive but be sure it is genuine. You might comment on, for example, how productive your relationship building was, the impact of your communication, or how the group could have better developed the assignment.

Many candidates find critical self-evaluation a challenge; we are all so used to hiding our weaknesses and promoting our strengths. But realize that otherwise very strong candidates fail because they have not been open enough about their weaknesses and have not taken the opportunity to describe the strategies they have devised to address them.

Presentations

There is a lot you can do before the day to prepare for your presentation.

1. Plan something to say on core issues relevant to most subjects

Every sector of industry has issues that are relevant to pretty well every scenario. They depend on the industry of course, but might include recent legislation, the environment, health and safety, equality of opportunity, inclusiveness of people with disabilities (don't only think wheelchairs but include all types of disability) and social inclusion generally. There are bound to be cross-cutting themes relevant to the organization to which you have applied, so research them. The opportunity may arise where you can refer to these issues and gain valuable points.

2. Decide in advance how you might structure your presentation

You are unlikely to know the subject of your presentation until a short time before you have to make it, but this does not mean that you cannot do some preparation on the possible structure you intend to use. In the introduction you may want to summarize what you intend to go on to say and then in your conclusion review what you have said. There are some very good publications on the making of successful presentations; they may be worth a look.

You might decide to start by stating succinctly the assignment and go on to describe why addressing the issue is useful or necessary. If appropriate you could then review the file material (people, budget, rules) or background. Headings after that point might include Actions, Recommendations, Alternatives and Conclusion. Do not forget that it is essential that you show enthusiasm throughout.

3. Practise getting your timing right

You may not yet know how long you will have to present, but all the same it is worth practising how much you can say effectively in the usual time slots allocated in these exercises. On the day you will be allocated something between 10 and 20 minutes and you do not want to finish short or overrun. To get it right you need to have some experience of how long it will take to present a series of points with impact. Try to say too much or too little and you may end up dis-appointed with your presentation. Listen to a few public speakers on the radio for example, and study how they make a point with impact and how long it takes them. You do not want to find yourself unable to cover all the points you planned to make and to be told to stop before you have made your concluding remarks.

4. The briefing and preparation time

You are often given a number of subjects from which to choose and are always provided with a briefing pack on the subject and told the time you have to prepare your presentation. Don't make the mistake of thinking you have to comment on all the subjects, including the ones you did not select. So, at the briefing, get absolutely clear in your mind the nature of the assignment and if in doubt ask someone for clarification. Be warned that it is common for the amount of time allowed for studying the background papers to be very tight. These events are sometimes organized so that the time allowed for reading the papers and preparing your presentation are combined, so be very careful not to spend too much time reading the papers and finding yourself with insufficient time to prepare your presentation.

Be sure to present the difficulties as well as the advantages of your approach to the topic. Often you are asked to provide some-thing original on the subject. Even if you are not specifically asked to do this, it may be worth offering a novel aspect to you presenta-tion and then go on to examine the benefits and challenges to this aspect (don't forget to identify it as an original contribution). The relevance of everything you say should be clear or be explained. In practice, the invigilators don't so much care what you decide on but judge you on how you explain, justify and criticize it.

Once you have decided what to say settle on your structure and make clear, legible notes to which you can refer when making the presentation, and resolve to keep to it. Allocate an amount of time to each part of your presentation. Do not try to write out verbatim what you hope to cover. Even if you could manage it in the time allowed, the exercise is not one of reading your essay out loud. Instead, try numbering your points and commit these numbers and key words belonging to the points to memory. Try labelling them with one-word reminders and memorizing these. Try anything that works for you and will help you recall the points you want to make without excessive reference to your notes.

Remember to work quickly, as you may find you have very little time to prepare for your presentation.

5. Your presentation

Nerves aside, your presentation is likely to be as good or bad as your preparation, both before the day and during the preparation time. The invigilator is not expecting a polished public performance, but do be sure to speak clearly, make eye contact and try to keep reference to your notes to a minimum. Think on your feet and adapt what you say as you speak, then revert back to your structure. Keep an eye on the time and try as much as possible to keep to the limits you set to speaking on each part of your presentation. If you find yourself going over time, drop some points. As already said, it is important to deliver a timely presentation and avoid being asked to stop before you have reached your conclusions. You are very likely to get the opportunity to raise further points and add details in the question and answer session that follows.

6. Follow-up questions/discussion

In these exercises it is common for more time to be spent answering questions and discussing what you said with the invigilator than you spent making your presentation.

It will help if you think of this time more as a brainstorming session than a cross-examination, so approach it with an open, curious mind rather than risk being perceived as defensive. During questions, invigilators may follow up your response and keep asking follow-up questions until they feel they have the measure of you. At some point they will have decided whether you have made the grade, but they may still keep asking questions until you run out of things to say. Don't let this undermine your self-confidence and don't take offence. When the next line of questioning begins, it's a fresh start, a new line of enquiry, and you should have a different line of responses. Avoid falling back to a previous response, ie avoid repeating yourself. At all times make sure your response is relevant to the question and the line of enquiry. Listening skills are as important here as they are in the group exercise. Expect there to be one person who leads the questions and one or more others who mainly observe and take notes.

7. Self-assessment

If you are required to complete a self-assessment of your performance in the presentation exercise then take it seriously and complete it to the best of you ability; a score of what you write may feature as a part of your overall assessment. See the note on self-assessment, above.

Written exercises

1. Overview

These are tests of your ability to handle information, organize it and communicate in writing. You will be presented with a file of papers that provide information on a subject. It may include conflicting information that you have to evaluate and make recommendations about. Your task is to analyse the papers and prepare a note that builds a balanced and convincing case. To do this you will need to compare and contrast the options, using the stated criteria or proposing your own, and explain convincingly the reasons for your recommendation. These exercises are nearly always completed on a computer, so make sure your keyboard skills are up to scratch.

2. Planning in advance

Again, you can undertake some useful preparation before the day. One thing to consider is the style of approach that you adopt. This decision will depend in part on your background and your strengths; it is obvious that you should play to these. It should also be dependent on the role for which you are applying. By this I mean, if you are applying for a role in business then adopt a business style of report writing, with an executive summary stating the recommendation and summarizing the whole document, the main body and then the conclusion. If you are applying to an academic institution then a university style of report may be more appropriate and, if you can, adopt an elegant, fluid, readable written style. Research on the internet the style of reports and publications used in the organization or industrial sector in which it operates and, if you are confident to do so, adopt this style in the written exercise. That way you will appear well suited to the position. If producing a written document is really not your thing, consider using (but not excessively) bullet points and underlined headings to help convey you message. Illustrate points, where applicable: they will be far more convincing. If you find that you have not included figures, you have probably not done as well as you could, so where practical back up and provide numerical evidence for what you say. Many organizations are looking for you to provide evidence of the case or point you make, so refer to figures or passages in the background paper and remember to reference sources.

Before the day it may be useful to give thought to analytical tools or processes to which you might refer or use in the exercise. Some have already been mentioned, including SWOT and PEST (see above). Consider if there are any core issues to which you might make reference in your paper that are applicable to most issues in the industrial sector to which you are applying. Look at reports and studies on the internet to identify possible issues. They might include, for example, equality of opportunity, reaching the hard to reach or challenging members of our society, or the contributions and/or threats technological advances might bring.

A common question asked is, how much should I write? The answer is that, within reason, what matters is not how much you write but what you write. Some assignments stipulate the extent expected, others do not. When no extent is indicated, set out to write enough to get the job done well. Don't write without good purpose, and take care to use the correct grammar, spelling and punctuation. Write too much and you increase the risk of errors and have less time to find any you may have made.

3. The briefing and preparation time

When you come to take the assignment it is very likely that you will be briefed on the exercise and provided with background or briefing papers. You may have a lot of information to go through and the time allowed to complete this part of the task may be tight. Be sure not to get caught out by the time limit. Get clear the aim of the exercise as explained to you and, first and foremost, use the time allowed to obtain the information necessary to serve the objective of the assignment. Then set about deciding the line to take in your paper and the structure that you will adopt.

4. The written assignment itself

Much of what you have done during your education and working career to date will serve you well in a written exercise. Take confidence from the fact that you have the skill to succeed in this assessment and apply what you have prepared before the day and during the briefing and preparation time. Although the written assignment is almost certainly to be administered on a PC, think back to the written exams at school or university for an idea of what to expect and insight into the best approach. Start with a note of the structure that you have decided to adopt and then use your time to implement that plan. Take care over grammar and spelling. Remember the invigilators are looking to see how well you can structure an argument and examine a number of options, recommending one. Where appropriate, use illustrations to make your points; back up what you say with figures; summarize rather than quote from the background information, paraphrasing it or restating the passage in your own words. Demonstrate your ability at handling numerical information by offering clear, succinct restatements of relevant data in the background information. Remember to reference sources. Be convincing while remaining impartial and objective.

Decision analysis

These assessments are about making good judgements in less than ideal circumstances – as is often the case in real life and work. The information provided is deliberately incomplete and the rules being followed are deliberately ambiguous. It is your task to decipher the code and then, despite the fact that the information is incomplete and that there is uncertainty, decide which of the suggested answers are best. You have to do this within a tight time frame.

Decision analysis belongs to the new generation of test types and is used to select for postgraduate courses and managerial training programmes. They are used, for example, to select candidates for medical and dental school. Practise with these questions if you face any of the various decision analysis sub-tests that exist. The task involved in the assessment that you face may differ in a number of important respects to the practice here, but still complete it because you will develop transferable competencies that will help you perform well in any assessment of your decision analysis skills.

This section comprises 50 practice questions. You are provided with a list of codes and their corresponding meanings. The code is followed by questions and each question involves a sequence of code and a series of suggested answers. In some instances more than one suggested answer is correct: you are always informed if you are to identify more than one best fit. It is your task to identify which of the suggested answers is or are the best interpretation of the code. Note that the sequence of codes can be used in a different order from that in which they are presented in the question. So, for example, the code xx (meaning rock) and yy (meaning paper) can be used to correctly construct the interpretation rock, paper or paper, rock. Also note that other words (not covered by the code) can be added to the suggested answer and it can still be correct. For example, it would be correct to translate the code xx, yy as rock and paper, paper or rock and so on. Pay particular attention to the commas in the questions. If two codes are not separated by a comma then they relate to each other and only each other. If the codes are separated by commas then they may relate to any of the other codes in the given sequence.

Notice that the list of codes includes two types: one entitled transfers or modifiers and a lexis or dictionary of words. The modifier transforms a word. For example, if a question states 'Reverse popular', then you need to find a word in the suggested answers that is the reverse of popular such as unpopular.

Try the following examples and allow yourself one minute for each question. Remember that you must select one best answer unless otherwise stated.

1. Codes

Transformers
311. Equivalent
312. Enlarge
313. Turn around
314. Decrease

Language
101. Vegetable
102. Oil
103. Octane
104. Alcohol
105. Ethanol
106. Gasoline
107. Diesel
108. Alternative
109. Investment
110. Bio

111. Fuel	113. Know
112. Tell	
521. New	524. Green
522. High	525. Gain
523. Few	526. More
731. Can	733. May
732. Could	734. Contradiction

Q1 733, 102, 312 522

    A. The price of oil is soaring.

    B. Gasoline prices may go sky high.

    C. He thinks oil futures may be sky-scraping.

    D. His views on oil may be well wide of the mark.

                                 Answer [   ]

Q2 311 734, 109, 111, 524

    A. There is disagreement over how good an investment green fuel is.

    B. He voiced opposition to the investment in bio fuel.

    C. Agreement was reached that green fuel was a good investment.

    D. Investment in green fuel is inconsistent.

                                 Answer [   ]

Q3 312 521, 313 113

    A. He is unaware of our innovative new product line.

    B. She can only guess at the novel approach.

    C. It's fresh and they are unaware.

    D. She could recognize the potential of the product.

                                 Answer [   ]

Q4 313 524, 103, 522, 111

A. Green fuel is high octane.

B. High-octane fuel is not green.

C. High-octane fuels are more polluting.

D. Few experienced drivers would select high-octane fuel.

Answer [ ]

Q5 106, 107, 113, 314 523

A. A tiny amount of ethanol is found in diesel.

B. Did you know diesel contains a few drops of ethanol?

C. A minority of people know diesel contains ethanol.

D. Very few know that most diesel contains ethanol.

Answer [ ]

Q6 111, 109, 313 108

A. Futures in conventional fuel are a good investment.

B. Mainstream banks invest in fuel stock.

C. Investment in unconventional fuel is growing.

D. Investment in alternative fuel supplies is growing.

Answer [ ]

Q7 Which two suggested answers best fit the code?
311 732, 104, 112, 524

A. Tell Mr Green alcohol might kill him.

B. It possibly will beat green sales of alcohol; only time will tell.

C. Tell him the alcohol is coloured green.

D. Alcohol as a green energy source might well take off.

Answer [ ]

Q8 312 112, 102, 101, 107

    A. Televise the fact that vegetable oil is an alternative to diesel.

    B. Diesel engines can run on vegetable oil.

    C. Say that diesel is better for the engine than vegetable oil.

    D. They hope their broadcasts will mean vegetable oil out-sells diesel.

Answer [   ]

Q9 522, 523, 113, 733

    A. Maybe it is high time a few people spoke out.

    B. You know only the high-flying few may gain more.

    C. I know a few who may have a high opinion of him.

    D. The risk may well be high but who can really know?

Answer [   ]

Q10 313 734, 314 521, 525

    A. The news is that the opposition party could gain two seats.

    B. They were in agreement of the gain made in fuel efficiency by recent designs.

    C. Modern systems gain much because they comply with quality standards.

    D. The latest efforts to harmonize trading standards are expected to gain approval.

Answer [   ]

2. Codes

Modifiers

321. Parallel	324. Lessen
322. Append	325. Akin
323. Reverse	326. Plural

Lexis

601. Elevated.	606. Add
602. Temperate	607. Delete
603. Tiny	608. Against
604. Popular	609. Deflation
605. Unfashionable	
930. Service	937. Pasta
931. Commodity	938. Mobile phone contract
932. Wide-screen TV	939. Refrigerator
933. Milk	940. Wooden flooring
934. Cigarettes	941. Gasoline
935. Banking	942. Soft furnishings
936. Landscaped gardening	943. The basket of goods
944. Piece	and services

Q11   321 602, 322 933

     A. That was a pleasant strawberry milkshake.

     B. Bottled milk is less popular today.

     C. Yogurt made from skimmed milk has less flavour.

     D. Can I have some cold custard?

                          Answer [   ]

Q12   Which code best fits:
Miniscule pasta pieces are unpopular?

     A. 321 944, 609, 938, 324 937, 604

     B. 934, 324 603, 323 604, 326 944

     C. 324 603, 937, 326 944, 323 604

     D. 324 603, 937, 326 323 604

                          Answer [   ]

Q13 322 607, 931, 604

    A. They may be popular but cigarettes are deadly.

    B. The most popular cigarettes are responsible for most smoking-related deaths.

    C. Cigarettes are popular but kill.

    D. Cigarettes should be banned.

                            Answer [ ]

Q14 933, 323 939

    A. Cook the milk.

    B. Put the milk in the microwave oven.

    C. Put the milk in the ice box.

    D. Heat the milk.

                            Answer [ ]

Q15 326 321 944

    A. Which bit is broken?

    B. The wide-screen TV was in bits.

    C. Do you have the set?

    D. The tiny parts were lost.

                            Answer [ ]

Q16 604, 324 942

    A. The popular table is this one.

    B. The popular choice is these curtains.

    C. The popular item is this set of beach towels.

    D. The sofa was the most popular.

                            Answer [ ]

Q17 323 606, 322 936

    A. The institute of landscape gardening planned to take away his membership.

    B. The landscape gardener removed his equipment.

    C. The landscape looked much better minus the rubbish dump.

    D. The landscape gardening company's accounts were in the red.

         Answer [   ]

Q18 321 930, 321 601

    A. The overhaul was long overdue.

    B. The important examination took place.

    C. The eminent bishop led the service.

    D. The prominent professor rose to speak.

         Answer [   ]

Q19 Which two suggested answers best fit the code?
324 938, 321 931, 325 605

    A. Mobile products soon become obsolete.

    B. Phone services are passé.

    C. These goods and services are unfashionable.

    D. Defunct products are rubbish.

         Answer [   ]

Q20 325 324, 323 609, 321 941, 608

    A. Cooking gas price rises are hurting the poor.

    B. Don't bank on oil prices not increasing.

    C. Banks are against the deflation of oil prices.

    D. Insure against aviation fuel inflation.

         Answer [   ]

3. Codes

Modifiers

201. Past	204. Reverse
202. Similar to	205. Contract
203. Same as	206. Expand

Vocabulary

310. He or She	321. Prefers
311. We	322. High
312. Know	323. Seems
313. Online	324. Looks
314. Try	325. Proves
315. Steal	326. No
316. Information	327. Only
317. Staff	328. If
318. Believe	329. Works
319. All	330. Week
320. Ready	

Q21 201, 324, 313, 310

    A. He looked online last week.

    B. She viewed the online information.

    C. He or she surfed the site only last night.

    D. She looked online yesterday.

Answer [＿＿＿＿＿＿]

Q22 Which two suggested answers best fit the code?
202 317, 315, 204 322

    A. Short members of the gang would pose as children and try to catch people off guard.

    B. Employees on low wages are far more likely to steal.

    C. The team only stole low-value items.

    D. Workers were advised to squat down in the event of an armed raid.

Answer [＿＿＿＿＿＿]

Q23 318, 328, 320, 205 318

    A. If you believe your estimate is ready then send it.

    B. Do you believe it or simply guess it is ready?

    C. I presume it is ready if you say so.

    D. If you believe so, fine; otherwise it is mere speculation.

                    Answer [　　　　　]

Q24 202 326, 323, 327

    A. I only ever seem to get a refusal.

    B. A negative seems only to make him more determined.

    C. It seems they are in denial.

    D. It seems like an affirmative is the only answer they accept.

                    Answer [　　　　　]

Q25 Which code best fits:

It's an inside job; he steals information while at work?

    A. 202 329, 329, 310, 316

    B. 202 329, 310, 316, 202 329

    C. 202 329, 316, 312

    D. 202 329, 329, 310, 312

                    Answer [　　　　　]

Q26 204 321, 330, 328

    A. The poor kid detests exams and has them all next week.

    B. They asked for rain but it has not stopped for a week.

    C. If his grandmother loathes something then watch out for a week.

    D. They dislike it intensely if their parents fight.

                    Answer [　　　　　]

Q27 201 318, 205 319

    A. He accepted a good few things as true.

    B. I suppose several theories might explain it.

    C. Everyone believed her.

    D. I thought that a number of times.

Answer

Q28 206 322, 310, 323

    A. He seems vastly overrated.

    B. It seems she is finding it an uphill struggle.

    C. She seems very nice.

    D. It seems straightforward but it's in fact a massive problem.

Answer

Q29 Which two suggested answers are the best fit?
329, 202 326

    A. If it works don't fix it.

    B. Going into the old steelworks is forbidden.

    C. His works are banned in many countries.

    D. The author of the works is unknown.

Answer

Q30 Which suggested answer is the least good fit?
204 311, 310

    A. He alone is responsible.

    B. As for myself I would rather not say.

    C. He and I have some history.

    D. She did it single-handed.

Answer

4. Codes

Converters

81. Equivalent   84. Decrease
82. Enlarge   85. Similar
83. Turn around

Key terms

221. Doubtful   229. Public
222. Reform   230. Better
223. Industry   231. Must
224. Children   232. Exceed
225. Rich   233. Education
226. Dishonest   234. Report
227. Result   235. Accept
228. Crucial   236. Merit

Q31 Identity the two suggested answers that best fit the code:
81 234, 84 230

A. The bulletin was highly critical.

B. An adequate account is all they could expect of the report.

C. The news was ok.

D. The demolition expert judged the explosion to be adequate.

Answer _____

Q32 225, 84 226, 231

A. There must be something wrong with a system where the rich pay proportionally less tax than the poor.

B. Some people get rich by questionable means.

C. It's a bit rich to say now that he must have cheated.

D. To prove her innocence she had to demonstrate how she got so rich by legal means.

Answer _____

Q33 223, 224, 83 235

    A. It was acknowledged that some children were found employed in the clothes industry.

    B. The education industry aims to eliminate underachieving children.

    C. The findings reject the claim that the toy industry exploits children.

    D. The childcare industry representatives refuse to attend.

Answer [＿＿＿＿＿]

Q34 Identity the two suggested answers that fit the code?
85 229, 81 228

    A. Open government has its critics.

    B. The support of the community was decisive.

    C. It is important that the newsletter is impartial.

    D. Key issues facing the civic authority were raised.

Answer [＿＿＿＿＿]

Q35 221, 81 236

    A. The worth of it all was doubtful.

    B. Some thought it a good point, others were doubtful.

    C. He doubted if there was any real advantage.

    D. Whether or not the result represented good value was doubtful.

Answer [＿＿＿＿＿]

Q36 83 225, 84 231, 228

    A. It is crucial that they should help the poor.

    B. The well-to-do who recognize their debt are crucial to our cause.

    C. We must advise the poor to expect more.

    D. The discontentment felt by the not-so-well-off has to be encouraged.

Answer [＿＿＿＿＿]

Q37 Which of the suggested answers best describes the statement: Commerce is corrupt?

A. 223, 83 226

B. 81 225, 82 221

C. 84 223, 82 228

D. 81 223, 81, 226

Answer [   ]

Q38 Which codes, if added to the list, would make it a good fit for the sentence: The reform of public services is decisive?
222, 229, 228

A. 84

B. 81

C. 83

D. 234

Answer [   ]

Q39 82 225, 84 225

A. The children of the hard-up dream of being prosperous.

B. Being underprivileged is something the wealthy look down on.

C. Better to be affluent today and needy tomorrow.

D. The moneyed and well-to-do have most to fear.

Answer [   ]

Q40 Which two suggested answers best fit the codes?
233, 224, 81 236

A. An education for all children is a right.

B. The education of our children is worth the price.

C. The advantage of an education for all children will exceed expectations.

D. No value can be placed on the benefits of an education for all our children.

Answer [   ]

5. Codes

Modifiers

99. Expand	101. Reverse
100. Reduce	102. Similar to

Terms

222. Makes	231. Smith
223. Unique	232. Million
224. Buy	233. Stamps
225. Small	234. Sold
226. Feature	235. Minus
227. Price	236. Investment
228. Twenty	237. Any
229. Cheap at	238. Bid
230. Collectors	239. Under

Q41 102 224, 231

    A. Smith bought twenty.

    B. Tell Smith to get as many as possible.

    C. Tell Smith to sell.

    D. Tell Smith to sell at any price.

Answer [ ]

Q42 99 225, 102 223

    A. The difference may be tiny but it is still very unusual.

    B. It's immensely important and atypical.

    C. That rare difference makes it immensely collectable.

    D. To find one so petite is odd.

Answer [ ]

Q43 230, 99 232

    A. Collectors will bid millions.

    B. In a million years collectors won't exist.

    C. There are millions of collectors of stamps.

    D. Several collectors will offer millions.

Answer [＿＿＿＿＿]

Q44 102 226, 102 238

    A. What attribute makes the proposal special?

    B. He has made an offer.

    C. Submit the final proposal.

    D. Make the tender private and confidential.

Answer [＿＿＿＿＿]

Q45 Which two sentences are a good fit for?
227, 102 235?

    A. It's price less.

    B. The price is not as much as others have sold for.

    C. There are very few in existence.

    D. There are fewer than three known examples hence the high price.

Answer [＿＿＿＿＿]

Q46 Which word if added to the list of codes would make the following sentence fit: That makes them cheap at any price?
229, 237, 227

    A. 230

    B. 223

    C. 222

    D. 234

Answer [＿＿＿＿＿]

Q47 234, 101 239, 232

    A. One sold years ago for more than a million.

    B. It sold for below a million.

    C. One sold for in excess of a million.

    D. It sold for over a million.

Answer ☐

Q48 Which code best fits the sentence: Stamps make good investments?

    A. 233, 100 222, 99 236

    B. 236, 222, 233

    C. 99 236, 100 233, 222

    D. 99 237, 236, 222

Answer ☐

Q49 Which two sentences are the best fit for the codes?
230, 224, 233, 236

    A. Stamps are considered a good investment which is why there are so many collectors.

    B. Collectors also buy stamps as an investment.

    C. Some collectors buy stamps to collect others as an investment.

    D. Some collectors will buy any stamp as an investment.

Answer ☐

Q50 99 228, 100 228

    A. In the last twenty years only one or two have come to the market.

    B. A few have sold for thousands of dollars.

    C. One of these went for more than a million.

    D. Three or four have fetched more than a thousand dollars apiece.

Answer

You will find many more decision analysis practice questions in the Kogan Page title, *How to Pass Advanced Verbal Reasoning Tests*, 2nd edition.

Verbal reasoning

I have applied for graduate schemes such as the NHS management, local government, civil service, and commercial banks. Most require the candidate to sit a verbal reasoning test. I found the 'true, false, cannot tell' comprehension questions to be challenging as the answers require certain judgement and inference especially choosing between 'false' and 'cannot tell'.

(A reader)

Your task in these common assessments is to read a passage and to determine in answer to a series of questions if the answer is true, false or that you cannot tell. The questions refer to the passage and require you to make accurate inferences, recognize assumptions, properly deduce, interpret information, evaluate arguments, comprehend meaning and significance, assess logical strength, identify valid inference, distinguish between a main idea and a subordinate one, recognize the writer's intention and identify a valid summary, interpretation or conclusion.

The subjects of the passages are drawn from a great many fields: current affairs, business, science, the environment, economics, history, meteorology, health or education. In fact, expect almost any subject matter. If you know something of the area then take care and do not bring your own knowledge to the passage. You are expected to answer the questions using only the information it contains. Be especially careful if you know a great deal about the subject or if you believe the passage to be factually incorrect or controversial. It is not a test of your general knowledge, your knowledge of the latest findings in the discipline or your political views. So feel at ease about answering true to a statement that is true in the very limited context of the passage but which you know to be false given what you learnt at university or read in a newspaper that morning. A few people err to the opposite extreme and are too strident in what they allow themselves to know. For example some candidates conclude they cannot know the meaning of everyday words unless a definition is provided in the passage. These assignments assume you are in full command of non-technical English and you are expected to demonstrate it.

If a verbal reasoning passage and the question lack provisos or qualification then answer true when it is clearly true, false when it is clearly untrue and cannot tell when it is not possible to answer true or false with certainty. If only it were always this simple! When publishers of real tests develop an advanced verbal reasoning test they rely on fine distinctions between the suggested answers in order to distinguish between the scores of the large numbers of candidates. These distinctions are sometimes much finer than those we draw on a day-to-day basis. As a result it is common for candidates to feel irritated and complain that these tests are to a large extent arbitrary. In a way they are; after all, this is not how we use language at work or anywhere other than in the surreal world of tests. This is something you just have to accept and get used to and with practice you will get to recognize the subtle distinctions being drawn.

At the graduate and advanced management level a good many of the questions require an advanced strategy. Employers rely on these assignments to identify whether applicants can demonstrate good judgement in a situation where an extent of uncertainty exists. At the graduate/higher managerial level therefore you must answer true when it is reasonable to conclude from the information in the passage that the statement is true. Answer false when, given the information in the passage, it is an unreasonable conclusion to draw. Reserve cannot tell for when a true or false answer would require information that is not provided, for example when the passage does not cover the point or is contradictory or ambiguous to the extent that new information is required to answer true or false with a reasonable degree of certainty. If you wonder how you are to know what is reasonable then again you need to practise, get used to making the judgement calls expected by the test author/employer and bring your notion of reasonable in line with theirs.

Under the stress of the real assessment it is common for candidates to have difficulty in choosing between false and cannot tell. If you are one of these candidates, ask yourself each time 'is the conclusion unreasonable or does it lack a sufficient degree of certainty?' If you conclude the former, answer untrue and cannot tell for the latter. Some of the judgement calls are deliberately close: they're testing you! An employer does not want staff who are reluctant to make decisions or who sit on the fence. So if you still can't decide between false and cannot tell be sure to read the questions as carefully as you read the passage and learn to pick up the many clues provided in the wording. For example, if the question asks about 'a valid argument, inference or premise', or asks whether it is necessarily the case that ..., then apply a strict criterion of proof. However, if the question asks, for example, is it reasonable ... on the balance of probability, that ... might the author, for the most part, on the whole, as a rule/generally, largely/nearly/mainly, in the majority ...' then adjust your criterion accordingly and apply a less strict proof. The question author is likely to be examining if you can make decisions under less than clear circumstances. When the question includes such provisos take care not to shy away from making a judgement. This way you will guard against answering cannot tell excessively.

Below are 100 practice questions; if you need more then get hold of *How to Pass Advanced Verbal Reasoning Tests*, 2nd edition as it contains hundreds.

Passage 1

Sound

The perception of sound is one of the major senses used for feeding, detecting predators and other dangers, and communication. Most vertebrates have specialist organs for sensing sound; many also have specialist organs for producing it. In water and air, sound is a sequence of compression waves. To be heard these waves must be within the range and sufficiently strong. Sound is a mechanical wave and animals perceive sound mechanically. The senses of smell, taste and vision all involve chemical reactions, but the hearing system is based on physical movement. In mammals this involves an eardrum that vibrates in sympathy with sounds and transfers the sound via three small bones named the hammer, anvil and stirrup to the inner ear. Here the stirrup rests on another membrane which covers the cochlea, a long tube the inside of which is covered with tiny hairs each connected to a bundle of nerves. The sound travels down the cochlea and bends the hairs, which in turn excite the associated nerve fibres. Not all sounds are audible to all animals and each species has a range of normal hearing. The brain perceives the pattern of excited nerve fibres in the cochlea produced by sounds in the range of normal hearing in the same way it deals with the visual patterns on the retina. When a particular trait of stimuli is repeated and associated with something of interest then we learn to identify these stimuli as a sound produced by that interesting event. It might be a sound produced by another individual to communicate a threat or an opportunity. Sounds that we humans cannot normally hear are called either ultrasound or infrasound. An ultrasound is above the normal human range and infrasound is below it. Cetaceans communicate and hunt using infrasound (they also produce sound audible to humans). Bats navigate and hunt using ultrasound. For example, orca or killer whales produce a great number of different sounds from clicks of 0.1 to 80 kHz to pulsing screams in the range of 1 to 25 kHz. Scientists have established that each clan of orca has its own dialect and they can identify which clan an individual belongs to from the calls and sounds it produces.

Q1 The sense of hearing therefore is mechanical.

True

False

Cannot tell

Answer

Q2 By the term 'range' the author expressly means both the frequency and amplitude.

True

False

Cannot tell

Answer

Q3 It can be inferred from the passage that humans cannot normally hear sounds with the frequency 0.1 to 80 kHz to pulsing screams in the range of 1 to 25 kHz.

True

False

Cannot tell

Answer

Q4 Sound also travels through solids.

True

False

Cannot tell

Answer

Passage 2

Recent research has provided further stark evidence of the educational apartheid dividing the achievements of bright children from low- and high-income families. The study followed for many years the progress of a sample of almost 40,000 of the brightest children. Two-thirds were drawn from low-income families. The research found that almost all the able children from high-income families realized three or more 'A' grades in exams at the age of 18 years. But it was found that only one in four of the most able children from low-income families achieved similar grades. A bright child from a high-income family was found to have a one in two chance of gaining a place at one of the best universities. A bright child from a low-income family had only a one in 10 chance of gaining such a place. The bright children from high-income families were themselves very likely to enjoy a high income in their working life. A significant majority of the bright children from low-income families failed to earn above the national average wage. An acrimonious debate amongst political parties and educational commentators followed. Anger was voiced over the sheer waste of talent and the cost to the economy of failing to nurture so many of the nation's gifted children. The greatest criticism was directed at the schools responsible for their education. Most low-income children attend schools funded by the state and it was concluded that these institutions were badly failing bright pupils. The contrast in performance between state and private schools received renewed public scrutiny and was described as a first-class, second-class education system. This divide had been known about for many years; however, the new research portrayed it in a new and even worse light. In defence of the state schools some commentators pointed out the important contribution that home life makes to achievement. It was argued that a child needed parental encouragement and resources such as a quiet place to study, books and internet access if they were to realize their full potential and that many low-income families were unable to provide such an environment. Others pointed out the far higher level of funding enjoyed by private schools and the autonomy they enjoy with respect to key functions such as admissions and curriculum.

Q5   The effect of this inequality puts the low-income, bright child at a considerable disadvantage.

True

False

Cannot tell

Answer [   ]

Q6   The acrimonious debate was widespread.

True

False

Cannot tell

Answer [   ]

Q7   The findings of the research can be accurately summed up in terms of a divide between achievement in state and private education.

True

False

Cannot tell

Answer [   ]

Q8   It was concluded in the report that a child needed parental encouragement and resources such as a quiet place to study, books and internet access if they were to realize their full potential.

True

False

Cannot tell

Answer [   ]

Passage 3

Great Zimbabwe

The largest ancient structure in all Africa south of the Sahara desert is the ruin of a city once the capital of a large country. The city after which the modern state is named prospered between the 11th and 14th centuries but afterwards fell into decline and was eventually abandoned. The remains of the ruined city include walls and in particular the great enclosure made from walls 11 meters high. The rest of the site covers an area of 7km^2 and comprises a maze of high walls. All the walls are constructed from huge shaped stones that fit perfectly together without the need for mortar. The city served as royal palace, administrative centre and centre of trade. At its heyday it is estimated that 18,000 people were resident in the city. The European migrants who arrived in the 19th century sought to dominate and subjugate the peoples of southern Africa and take control of their territory. Whilst the European settlers intended to take permanently the lands and enslave or expel the native people they relied on their country of origin for economic and military assistance and offered in return their allegiance to their homeland. They relied on the army of their homeland to defend their homesteads and the judiciary to provide summary justice in the event of a crime committed against their property or person. They justified their actions on the basis that the land they had taken was wild and uncultivated. They dismissed the native people as uncivilized and beneficiaries of the 'development and progress' their imperialism brought. The existence of a highly developed city state dating back almost a thousand years threatened their justification so they either denied its existence or insisted that it could not have been a city populated and built by native people but the remains of a previous conquest and invasion.

Q9   The existence of the city confounded the 19th-century colonialist view of Africa.

True

False

Cannot tell

Answer [   ]

Q10 Great Zimbabwe is found in the modern state of Zimbabwe.

True

False

Cannot tell

Answer [   ]

Q11 The most striking feature of the ruined city is its walls.

True

False

Cannot tell

Answer [   ]

Q12 It can be inferred from the passage that the city was abandoned in the 14th century.

True

False

Cannot tell

Answer [   ]

Passage 4

Clouds

When the sun is shining down onto a cloud it appears white. A satellite image of the clouds shows them as white because the sun is shining down onto them. If the sun is behind the clouds it will appear dark. Sunlight that hits a cloud at a shallow angle may make the cloud appear silver, yellow or even red. Clouds are made of visible condensed water vapour and form because warm air close to the earth absorbs water moisture and this water-laden air tends to rise. As it rises it cools and as it reaches saturation temperature the water vapour condenses and becomes visible. The exception to this is fog. Fog is a thick cloud of water droplets at or near ground level. It occurs where the saturated air has not risen or once risen descends. Clouds are named according to their shape. Flat clouds are called stratus, feathery clouds cirrus. When looking up to the clouds we can read a good deal of information from them about the attendant or approaching weather. A dramatic example is a thunderstorm. Thunderstorms are storms with thunder and lighting and typically very heavy rain. They are always associated with cumulonimbus clouds. These are huge clouds stretching as much as 9 km into the sky with a distinctive anvil-shaped top. As they approach they appear dark and menacing and bring very localized and extreme weather. You can sometimes watch a thunderstorm cloud forming or to describe it better, swelling upwards, usually in the evening. A much more welcome cloud is the cumulus because small or medium-sized cumuli are typically present during periods of fine settled weather. They are easily recognized as the knobby, fluffy clouds most children draw in their pictures and look like irregularly shaped balls of cotton wool.

Q13 It would be false to describe cumulus clouds as lumpy.

True

False

Cannot tell

Answer

Q14 Clouds do sometimes have colour and it depends on the angle from which the sun is shining onto them.

True

False

Cannot tell

Answer

Q15 From a satellite image of the clouds we can map out the current weather systems.

True

False

Cannot tell

Answer

Q16 We can think of fog as a cloud resting on the ground.

True

False

Cannot tell

Answer

Passage 5

A pension is a regular payment made to someone during their retirement or a period of infirmity. The payments are made by either
the state to which the person has paid contributions in order to
qualify or from an investment fund that the person has built up
during their working life. A third group of people are in schemes in
which their employer also makes a contribution but most of these
people are not troubled by the issues identified here. Purportedly,
we face a pensions crisis because more than half of all working
people will rely solely on the state to provide a pension in their old
age. These people have paid into a state pension scheme all their
working lives. In return they expect to be provided with a state pension on which to live during their old age. Why then talk of a crisis?
In the 1960s there was one pensioner for every five workers; this
ratio has dropped to one pensioner for every three people in work
and is forecast to go as low as one to every two within the next 20
years. Should this happen the government will simply not be able to
live up to its commitments and provide pensions to the millions of
retired people. To make ends meet it is estimated that the government will have to cut the already low pension rate by 30 per cent.
This means that those who rely solely on the state for a pension
could find themselves retiring to utter poverty. It will directly affect
around 12 million people, so it is no wonder people are talking about
a crisis. A large slice of the other half of the working population is
also at risk of retiring to poverty. These workers have, as well as their
state pension, a private scheme to which they contribute and they
intend to use it to top up their state pension in retirement. However,
most are contributing only a pittance towards these schemes and
have funds currently valued at less than £10,000. Consequently on
their retirement most of these people will find that their private
schemes are insufficient to buy them a meaningful second source
of income.

Q17 The passage states that a pensioner is a person who receives a pension.

True

False

Cannot tell

Answer [   ]

Q18 The author uses the term 'purportedly' when he writes: 'Purportedly, we face a pensions crisis because more than half of all working people will rely solely on the state to provide a pension in their old age', raising the possibility that the claim that we face a crisis is false.

True

False

Cannot tell

Answer [   ]

Q19 Given that the 'large slice of the other half of the working population' has a private scheme that is insufficient, something like 20 million in total will be directly affected.

True

False

Cannot tell

Answer [   ]

Q20 12 million equals more than half of all working people.

True

False

Cannot tell

Answer [   ]

Passage 6

Physical properties of water

Our planet should really be called Water not Earth because water covers over 70 per cent of its surface. Water is essential for life and it is special as it has many unique or unusual properties. Take for example the fact that no other substance coexists naturally as a liquid, solid and gas on Earth's surface. Water has many other unique or unusual properties and these properties give us insight into the workings of our world. Another example is that water's density increases with salinity. This is why pure water (and freshwater) float on seawater. Pure water freezes at 0°C. The addition of salt lowers the freezing point. Seawater with an average salinity freezes at almost −2°C below that of the freezing point of pure water. The crystal structure of solid water is less dense than liquid water and this is why ice floats on water. Most solids have higher densities than their liquid forms so they sink in their own liquids, but not water. The maximum density of water is realized at a little below 4°C. The electrostatic bonding of water molecules requires a lot of heat to break the bond and this means that when water is heated its temperature rises relatively slowly and when cooled water releases a relatively large amount of energy for the decrease in temperature. For this reason water is said to have a high heat capacity and it means that the sea during the summer absorbs a great amount of heat which it releases during the winter. Water is also a uniquely powerful solvent. Virtually every substance dissolves in water to some extent. This is why seawater is found to contain a vast number of substances dissolved in it including trace amounts of most gases and metals. The two most plentiful solutes are chlorine and sodium ions. These two solutes account for seawater's most distinct quality: its salinity.

Q21 When the author wrote 'This is why pure water (and fresh-water) float on seawater' what he in fact meant was that solid pure or freshwater floats on seawater.

True

False

Cannot tell

Answer [　　　　　　]

Q22 That water's density increases with salinity is a unique quality.

True

False

Cannot tell

Answer [　　　　　　]

Q23 The author would agree water's most distinct quality is its salinity.

True

False

Cannot tell

Answer [　　　　　　]

Q24 The passage states that most solids have higher densities than their liquid forms so they sink in their own liquids, but not water. From this we can infer that an iron bar would sink if placed into molten iron.

True

False

Cannot tell

Answer [　　　　　　]

Passage 7

Encryption

Encryption is used in many more situations than espionage when governments encode secrets and spies pass coded messages written in invisible ink. In the digital world it has become imperative that we protect information and information systems from unauthorized access, modification, copying or theft and encryption has become the most popular form of information security. Credit card information, sensitive company information such as customers' personal records, details of bank account transactions and government information about citizens' health and tax records are routinely encrypted. Take for example ATMs: to prevent fraud it is required by law that sensitive data in ATM transactions is encrypted before being transmitted between the ATM and the bank processing centre. To encrypt the information an algorithm is used making it unreadable unless you possess the key to make it unencrypted or readable again. An algorithm is a set of rules that define a sequence of operations. The sequence can run for a very long time, possibly infinitely. Key to the use of an algorithm in encryption therefore is stating in advance the length of the sequence of operations because without this knowledge we cannot know the answer and unlock the code. There are countless examples of when data has been intercepted and stolen when in transit. Had that information been encrypted before it was sent then while it would still be intercepted it would be useless to the interceptor because they would find it unreadable. If data is encrypted before being stored and the key located somewhere else then if a laptop or flash drive is stolen or lost or someone gains unauthorized access to a network or copies data, it remains secure. There are a number of free encryption software programs available on the internet. Typically the program will encrypt entire folders or even whole hard drives; it then 'shreds' the original files after encryption so that they are no longer viewable and it hides the encrypted files so that someone unauthorized to access the data will not even realize they are there. Just don't forget your password because otherwise you will not be able to unencrypt your work. Imagine!

Q25 Hiding encrypted files is the information technology equivalent to a coded message written in invisible ink.

True

False

Cannot tell

Answer [   ]

Q26 In many countries it is law that certain information (for example ATM transactions) must be encrypted.

True

False

Cannot tell

Answer [   ]

Q27 Encryption is essential for businesses and government but is not something everyone needs or can afford.

True

False

Cannot tell

Answer [   ]

Q28 It has become vitally important that data is encrypted both when stored on hard drives or flash drives and before it is sent via the internet or across networks.

True

False

Cannot tell

Answer [   ]

Passage 8

Gaia theory

The novelist William Golding's first novel, *Lord of the Flies,* was published in 1954. The central theme of the book is the conflict between the desire to live morally and according to statutes against the instinct to satisfy one's urges and disregard the good of the group. Golding spent the war in the UK Royal Navy and saw considerable action. He spent many years working as a secondary school teacher. His first interest was science and he started his university studies reading it but he changed subject and graduated in English literature. At one stage in his remarkable life he lived next door to Professor James Lovelock and from this chance occurrence the Gaia theory was born. It was Golding who suggested the name Gaia, the Greek goddess of the Earth, for Lovelock's earth feedback hypothesis. According to ancient Greek legend Gaia was born out of chaos, a parthenogenic birth, and received as gifts the mountains and seas and all vegetation and animal life. Golding died in 1993. Lovelock is the author of four books, *The Gaia Theory, The Ages of Gaia, Homage to Gaia* (an autobiography) and most recently *The Revenge of Gaia.* The theory asserts that the planet Earth is a self-regulated living being and can be viewed as a single organism that automatically regulates temperature, ocean salinity and atmospheric content so as to keep conditions just right for life to continue. James Lovelock is in favour of the use of clean nuclear energy, respectful of the environment. Nuclear energy is reputed to be the method of energy generation with the lowest impact on the environment in terms of air pollutants and its footprint on the land it occupies. For these reasons many contemporary environmentalists acknowledge its potential contribution to sustainable economies.

Q29 It can be deduced from the passage that a parthenogenic birth is one that arises from chaos.

True

False

Cannot tell

Answer

Q30 In the most part Golding was sympathetic to Lovelock's Gaia theory.

True

False

Cannot tell

Answer

Q31 Golding's first novel was published 39 years after his death.

True

False

Cannot tell

Answer

Q32 Lovelock's latest book is entitled *The Revenge of Gaia* and his first *The Gaia Theory*.

True

False

Cannot tell

Answer

Passage 9

The printed word, the radio and television used to be the only sources of information available to a mass audience. Journalists and radio and television presenters were household names; they decided what we saw and heard and their opinions carried great authority. But people no longer passively consume media content and they are beginning to value their own opinion and offer it alongside that of the supposed experts and authorities. They post online ratings for the restaurants they visit, they share their home-made podcasts and videologs, they contribute entries to collaborative sites offering advice or answers to questions posed on every imaginable subject. They are quickly realizing that the experts and authorities have feet of clay and that only too often a rank amateur offers a more pro-found contribution to the debate. It is the beginning of an expressive revolution that has only recently become possible and will embrace most people in the future. Not every review or entry on the internet is correct and, sure, some are bizarre. But the same has always been true of the content of our daily newspapers or favourite radio pro-grammes. Audiences are receptive to many more versions of truth and are becoming adept editors deciding for themselves what is worthwhile and credible. The revolution is creating considerable pessimism amongst the employees of the traditional media corpor-ations as they realize the extent to which the business model to which they have become accustomed is threatened. They can barely believe that users might put as much or more onto the network as they download. How wrong they turned out to be.

Q33 The passage examines the ongoing expressive revolution that is predicted will embrace most people provided it is true that audiences are becoming adept editors deciding for them-selves what is worthwhile and credible.

True

False

Cannot tell

Answer [   ]

Q34 The author would most likely agree that the traditional media corporations had known all along that the internet would not simply be another outlet for their products.

True

False

Cannot tell

Answer

Q35 In the context of the passage the word expressive means animated.

True

False

Cannot tell

Answer

Q36 The author relies on examples but not analogies to make his case.

True

False

Cannot tell

Answer

Passage 10

Sea sickness

Cruise ship companies find that around 12 per cent of their passengers report vomiting due to seasickness. It is no coincidence that the word nausea comes from the Ancient Greek word 'naus' meaning ship. We seek to keep our centre of gravity over our feet and we rely on visual references and the balance organs in our inner ears to do this. Seasickness occurs when our visual reference to our surroundings and our balance organs are confused. This is why someone is more likely to feel seasick if, for example, they read a book while at sea even in seemingly calm conditions. Their senses are reporting conflicting information: their visual references report no motion while their balance organs report motion. The more violent the motion the faster the onset of seasickness and the greater likelihood that someone will show the symptoms. The resulting confusion brings on nausea and vomiting. Anxiety can make seasickness more likely. If someone is fearful of travel by ship or boat, then they are more likely to suffer from seasickness. If someone is tired they are also more likely to fall victim. Some people are particularly vulnerable to seasickness while others appear immune or become immune through exposure. When someone is seasick they can seem really unwell. Their complexion is pale; they may sweat and complain of feeling clammy. They may continue to retch even though their stomach is long empty. They are unsteady on their feet and may appear incoherent. The best thing for them to do is to lie down with their eyes closed and if possible sleep. This usually stops the symptoms. However, as soon as they awake and rise, the symptoms will return. Some sufferers are able to take small sips of water, allowing them to remain hydrated without further vomiting. Others are unable to do this without the onset of further sickness and these individuals are at risk of becoming dehydrated. There are a number of remedies for seasickness. Tablets are available that reduce nausea; however, many have the side effect of drowsiness and so are unsuitable. Some people find wrist bands that apply pressure to a point just above the wrist effective. Others prefer a slow-release patch that contains a drug that reduces nausea, at a dosage that does not risk bringing on sleepiness. The single best cure of seasickness, however, is to 'hug a tree'. There are no trees at sea, so in order to hug one and be cured of seasickness you must step ashore.

Q37 Anxiety and tiredness are contributory factors to the onset of seasickness.

True

False

Cannot tell

Answer [   ]

Q38 The author would agree with most experts that almost everyone will get seasick if the conditions are extreme enough.

True

False

Cannot tell

Answer [   ]

Q39 An acceptable alternative to the word 'confusion' in the passage would be disorder and perspective would be an acceptable alternative to 'complexion'.

True

False

Cannot tell

Answer [   ]

Q40 Could 'tablets are available that reduce nausea; however, many have the side effect of drowsiness and so are unsuitable' mean that they are unsuitable if the individual must operate equipment, serve passengers or sail the vessel?

True

False

Cannot tell

Answer [   ]

Passage 11

Puppetry

There are scores of forms of theatre: many ancient and a few found in almost all societies. Puppetry as a form of theatre originated in India many thousands of years ago. Clay puppets depicting people and animals have been excavated in the Indus Valley. There is archaeological evidence of a tradition of puppetry as a form of public entertainment in China too and that tradition is thought to go back to something like 2,000 years BC. To put on a puppet show requires relatively few resources but much skill. The reason puppetry is so universal derives from this: travelling puppet shows are easily arranged and such shows spread this form of art from India across the civilizations of Asia, Africa, Europe and even to pre-Columbus societies in Central America. The travelling puppet shows of Europe share their storylines with those played in India, confirming the theory that their heritage lies to the East. In China puppetry was watched by members of every strand of society. In Europe, however, it became associated with lower social classes where rough and ready puppet shows were shown in inns and taverns or set up on village greens and at country fairs. Perhaps the most elaborate and skilled puppet shows are found in Indonesia where again the storyline owes its heritage to the Indian tradition of puppetry. Even the casual observer will realize that puppetry has much in common and no doubt developed from children's play. Watch any child playing with a doll or toy animal and you are watching a sort of puppet show. This connection between childhood and puppetry as a form of public entertainment may well explain puppetry's incredible appeal and its ability to captivate an audience of all ages. The connection with childhood goes further because puppets are used to tell a story. When we watch a puppet show we are transported back to the magical world of childhood and the stories that we heard and made up in our play, so no wonder it has so great an appeal.

Q41 An example of a tradition of theatre that is both ancient and universal is puppetry.

True

False

Cannot tell

Answer

Q42 It is reasonable to infer that the storyline in Chinese puppetry owes its heritage to the Indian tradition.

True

False

Cannot tell

Answer

Q43 The people who walked across the land bridge from Asia to the Americas took puppetry with them.

True

False

Cannot tell

Answer

Q44 The author may accept as evidence of a tradition of puppetry as theatre an ancient clay doll with articulated head, arms and legs found in a child's tomb.

True

False

Cannot tell

Answer

Passage 12

The Arawaks

When Columbus first arrived in the Bahamas in the autumn of 1492 the first people he met were Arawak Indians. We do not know if in fact they called themselves Arawaks, on the occasion of the first meeting; this name dates from a later period and is another native American people's name for cassava flour. Columbus did not say if he established what they called themselves or if he did, he did not consider it worth recording. The Arawak people grew cassava as a staple and used it extensively in their cooking, religious ceremonies and festivals. They made a fermented drink from cassava flour. On the occasion of the first meeting between the people of the Caribbean and the Spanish, Columbus and his men exchanged balls of cotton and parrots for pieces of iron. He described them as 'primitive', without ferrous objects, who used stone and wooden tools and weapons and were 'easy to subjugate and make do (his) bidding'. His journals include very little information about the Arawaks but he became far more interested in conversing with them when he noticed that a few men had a small piece of gold hanging from a hole in their nose. He established from their signs that the gold was obtained from people to the south who it seemed had piles of it. He tried to get them to show him the way but he complained that they would not help him. He took seven of the men captive with the intention of having them lead him to the gold or if that plan failed he resolved to take them to Spain as a prize for the king. Some meaningful insight into the traditions of the Arawak people is obtained from the journals of settlers. From this record it can be established that the Arawak nation and people occupied the Bahamas, Greater and Lesser Antilles, Trinidad and the eastern coast of South America as far south as Brazil. A group of German pilgrim brothers landed on the island of Grenada in the 1630s and they wrote of the Arawak people they lived among. They wrote of how their cleanliness was far superior to their own, that the Arawak had no metals of their own and used tools and weapons expertly fashioned from stone and wood and that the men hunted and the women grew crops, prepared food and undertook all the chores. They lived in open-sided huts and wore simple clothes made from woven cotton. They slept in hammocks and were very polite towards each other and held the elders of their community in high regard. The pilgrims described them as hospitable people who considered it a privilege to share what they had. Within a few decades of the European arrival, smallpox and other diseases, combined with enslavement and enforced resettlement, meant that the Arawak populations of the Bahamas and most of the Greater and Lesser Antilles islands were annihilated. Recent DNA studies have established that a few full-blood Arawak populations remain in the Caribbean islands of Cuba and the Dominican Republic and on the Central American eastern coast.

Q45 Arawak may have been a name that another Caribbean people called the first people that Columbus met in the new world; we simply do not know.

True

False

Cannot tell

Answer ⬚

Q46 The passage contradicts itself when it is written that Columbus and his men exchanged balls of cotton and parrots for pieces of iron.

True

False

Cannot tell

Answer ⬚

Q47 Columbus wrote little of the culture, customs and language of the Arawak people.

True

False

Cannot tell

Answer ⬚

Q48 While a few full-blood Arawak populations remain, their language and culture are lost.

True

False

Cannot tell

Answer [   ]

Passage 13

Independence

Since 1603 Scotland and England have shared a monarch when King James VI of Scotland inherited the throne from Queen Elizabeth I of England. The event was called the Union of Crowns but in fact involved two crowns placed on one head. The two states remained autonomous and self-governing under a single monarch, each with their own parliaments and legislatures until they became joined (under the Act of Union) and each country's parliament passed Parliamentary Acts and the single United Kingdom of Great Britain was formed. On 1 May 1707 the Act of Union was effective and the Scottish and English Parliaments dissolved and the Parliament of Great Britain based in the Palace of Westminster in London was formed. The Act of Union passed almost without celebration on its tercentenary. However, there was considerable celebration in Scotland with the passing of the Scotland Act in 1998 by the Parliament of Great Britain which re-established a Scottish Parliament with devolved powers and it first sat in 1999. For the first time, some 11 years after it was re-established, the Scottish National Party (the political party that seeks Scottish withdrawal from the union) is set to take control of the devolved Scottish Parliament. This raises the question of how an independent Scotland might prosper. Much is made of the North Sea oil revenue, which if allocated entirely to Scotland would this year amount to more than £15 billion. This is by no means a typical year, however, as annual oil revenue has averaged nearer £7 billion. Other tax incomes total something in the region of £30 billion annually. Currently, annual expenditure in Scotland is estimated to be over £50 billion. To be more definite after so many years of unification is difficult. In any event, a people of 5 million may well be very willing to chance the consequences of independence and are certainly capable of demonstrating a dynamism that overcomes any cost and potential drawbacks of independence. Certainly this is the view of Scottish Nationalist politicians who believe it long past the time for the return of independence and time for the Scottish Parliament to once again become a fully sovereign parliament. They have never been able to take seriously the arguments against independence and argue that the people of Scotland are capable of making their country better and controlling all matters affecting their wellbeing.

Q49 Scotland was without its own parliament for 292 years.

True

False

Cannot tell

Answer [   ]

Q50 The Scottish National Party took control of the devolved Scottish Parliament in 2009.

True

False

Cannot tell

Answer [   ]

Q51 The ideal of an independent Scotland is only brought up in relation to modern times.

True

False

Cannot tell

Answer [   ]

Q52 The majority of Scots are in favour of independence for Scotland.

True

False

Cannot tell

Answer

CHAPTER 5

Attitudinal and personality questionnaires

This chapter comprises two sorts of practice questions. The first are typical personality questions: they are short statements and you have to say if you agree with them or not. Some people mistakenly believe that you cannot improve your performance in this style of assignment: they rush them and do not give the statements sufficient consideration. It is essential that you answer the questions truthfully but it is equally essential that you keep at the front of your mind the context of the question. You are applying for a position of employment or training so with each question ask yourself, 'As an applicant how would I respond in that situation?' Take for example the statement: 'I would describe myself as tactful.' You should be able to answer this question positively. You might be able to think up some situation when you would not describe yourself as tactful, perhaps when out with your friends or at home with your family. But this would be the totally wrong response in the context of the question. How you sometimes act with your friends or family is irrelevant to your professional approach. Some argue that these questions do not have a right or wrong answer because it depends on your and the employer's preferences and while this is true for many of the statements it is not true of them all and some most definitely have a wrong answer. Take for example the statement, 'It is acceptable to discriminate on the basis of someone's race.' This statement most definitely has a wrong answer and any candidate who agreed with it is very likely to have his or her application rejected. The other type of question reviewed below is typical of the sort you face in situational awareness sub-tests or what are sometimes called job simulation assessments. Usually you are presented with 25 workplace scenarios that you could face at work in a managerial position.

In the practice below, answer the first sort of question by indicating if you agree or disagree or agree/disagree strongly with the statement. In the case of the situation awareness practice, each question describes a scenario or situation followed by five options. You must indicate which of the options is the most preferred, the next most preferred and so on, and rank each option as A the most appropriate, B acceptable, and C as a less than acceptable response. This means that there are more options (five) than rankings (three) and you must rank more than one response the same. If you consider two or more options as the most appropriate then do not rank any as A instead rank them as B, an acceptable response. It is possible that you do not rate any of the responses as the most appropriate or as acceptable, in which case do not rank any as A or B but rank them all as C, less that acceptable.

Use this practice to prepare for a real assessment. Keep at the forefront of your mind the position for which you are applying and the likely culture of the sort of company in the industry of your choice. Ensure that you answer in a way that supports your application; in other words always answer the question in the context of how you would act if you were working for the company in the role for which you are applying.

There is no conflict between giving an honest response while presenting yourself in the best possible light. It is perfectly reasonable that you should stress some parts of your personality over others in response to your understanding of the organization's culture and preferred way of working.

Be prepared to make a number of responses that you know will not support your application: to do otherwise would involve making a misleading response. Everyone will answer some questions with low-scoring responses and it is rare for a few to determine the overall result. The exception to this is an attitudinal questionnaire where a single wrong response could result in your application being rejected if, for example, your response implied that you were racist, dishonest or off-hand about health and safety. Employers are increasingly using personality-style assessments to try to predict how applicants, once employed, might conduct themselves in the workplace. In this context the employer is trying to identify the potential employee who might have the wrong approach to, for example: health and safety, equal opportunities, the handling of a grievance or someone in a position of authority. You need to approach these questions carefully. In particular, you must avoid the wrong answers, by which I mean the suggested answers that could imply that you would act inappropriately in work and so should not be employed. In your current work you may well have a contract of employment and a number of policy documents that form a part of that contract. Read these documents before you complete a personality-style test as they will help you understand the responsibilities of an employee and what it is reasonable for an employer to expect of you. For example, the equal opportunities policy will describe how every employee can expect to work in an environment free of the fear of discrimination on the grounds of race, gender or disability and that it is every employee's responsibility to help ensure such an environment. The health and safety policy will require all employees to report immediately anything they consider to represent a danger. These conditions of employment are very similar across all employers. Use these responsibilities to inform how you would act in some of the workplace situations.

The two styles of question are mixed up in the practice below. The answer to many questions will depend on your and the employer's preferences and for this reason I have not always indicated a right answer. Where I am unable to provide an answer I have provided an explanation of what conclusions an employer is likely to draw from the question or issues you should consider while deciding your response.

Q1   A problem shared is a problem halved.

    A. Agree strongly

    B. Agree

    C. Do not agree or disagree

    D. Disagree

    E. Disagree strongly

Answer [ ]

Q2   My success is due to my full understanding of the market-place and competitors' trends.

    A. Agree strongly

    B. Agree

    C. Do not agree or disagree

    D. Disagree

    E. Disagree strongly

Answer [ ]

SITUATION 3

You are the only black person in the company and you believe you are being treated differently to your colleagues because you are only offered the unpopular shifts and denied the overtime everyone else is offered. Your fears were confirmed when colleagues started calling you names that are obviously a reference to your ethnic origin. Your confidence is low, you felt humiliated and physically sick.

Q3 Rate the suggested responses as: A. The most appropriate response; B. An acceptable response; C. A less than acceptable response.

The suggested responses:

1. Say and do nothing because if you do not react the name-calling will fail in its purpose and people will get bored with it.

2. Talk to colleagues who might be suffering the same problems and if they are, work out together what you can do about it.

3. Keep a diary of events of who said what, when, the circumstances and any witnesses. This will give a vital record of the nature of the racism you are facing.

4. Find out whether your employer has specific rules about racism at work or a grievance procedure you can use to raise the issue and try to solve the problem.

Your answer:

1. ____

2. ____

3. ____

4. ____

Q4 Drive and determination are the keys to my success.

A. Agree strongly

B. Agree

C. Do not agree or disagree

D. Disagree

E. Disagree strongly

Answer [   ]

Q5 Success comes to a great team empowered by exemplary management.

A. Agree strongly

B. Agree

C. Do not agree or disagree

D. Disagree

E. Disagree strongly

Answer [   ]

Q6 My success is due to my ability to think strategically while overseeing day-to-day activities.

A. Agree strongly

B. Agree

C. Do not agree or disagree

D. Disagree

E. Disagree strongly

Answer [   ]

SITUATION 7

The work is dirty, the washing facilities are rudimentary and there is nowhere to store your clothes so that you can wear the provided protective clothing. Nor is there an area for rest breaks and to eat meals. So you stand around outside during breaks and eat where you can; when it rains you all get wet. None of your co-workers are women and the general public are not allowed on site so you don't believe there is any need to provide somewhere private to get changed or suitable facilities for pregnant women or nursing mothers. However, you do believe that your employer should provide better facilities or at least some sort of facilities. You have discussed this with him more than once but you are just dismissed as a troublemaker.

Q7 Rate the suggested responses as: A. The most appropriate response; B. An acceptable response; C. A less than acceptable response.

The suggested responses:

1. Try talking informally again with your employer about the inadequate working conditions.

2. Do nothing because only businesses employing five or more people must have facilities for staff to change, rest and eat.

3. Refuse to work until facilities are improved and not worry about being threatened with disciplinary action because an industrial tribunal would be bound to agree that conditions were inadequate.

4. Raise the matter in writing with your employer, outlining your concerns and how you believe things might be arranged differently.

Your answer:

1. ____

2. ____

3. ____

4. ____

Q8 My success is due to my strong interpersonal skills.

A. Agree strongly

B. Agree

C. Do not agree or disagree

D. Disagree

E. Disagree strongly

Answer [   ]

Q9 My success is due to my ability to think laterally and outside the box.

A. Agree strongly

B. Agree

C. Do not agree or disagree

D. Disagree

E. Disagree strongly

Answer [   ]

Q10 It is better to double margins than the customer base.

A. Agree strongly

B. Agree

C. Do not agree or disagree

D. Disagree

E. Disagree strongly

Answer [   ]

SITUATION 11

I have a few strong beliefs especially when it comes to the welfare of animals, but this does not normally affect my working relationship with colleagues. Last week, however, during a tea break I found myself in a heated argument when a colleague said it was ok to drown unwanted kittens in a bucket. Things got a bit out of hand and I guess we all said things we didn't really mean. Except for essential work-related communication we have not spoken since. I feel upset and stressed by the situation and it is affecting my work.

Q11 Rate the suggested responses as: A. The most appropriate response; B. An acceptable response; C. A less than acceptable response.

The suggested responses:

1. I would try to resolve things informally with my co-workers and if it did not work then I would next raise the matter informally with my supervisor to see if she could help resolve matters.

2. The first thing I would do is write a letter to my employer setting out the details of the grievance I have with my co-workers.

3. I would ask my employer if I could be transferred to another section and if this was not possible I would tender my resignation.

4. I would try talking with my employer informally to see if there was anything they could do to improve the situation. If that did not work I would raise a formal grievance against my colleagues.

Your answer:

1. ____

2. ____

3. ____

4. ____

Q12 Getting on in business requires ruthlessness.

A. Agree strongly

B. Agree

C. Do not agree or disagree

D. Disagree

E. Disagree strongly

Answer [   ]

Q13 I might lack some of the years of experience offered by other candidates but my success comes from the energy and determination that I have to make things happen.

A. Agree strongly

B. Agree

C. Do not agree or disagree

D. Disagree

E. Disagree strongly

Answer [   ]

SITUATION 14

You're organizing a day-long conference and the chief executive of your company will be attending. Ultimately the success of the day is your responsibility. Everything is going to plan until the catering company informs you at the last minute that they forgot to ask about the chief executive's food preferences. Upon checking, you find out that she is a vegetarian and there's no suitable food for her. The chief executive is due to sit down to lunch very shortly.

Q14 Rate the suggested responses as: A. The most appropriate response; B. An acceptable response; C. A less than acceptable response.

The suggested responses:

1. Tell the most senior member of the catering company present that they must immediately locate a meal suitable for the chief executive.

2. Run outside and buy a vegetarian lunch for the chief executive yourself.

3. Send a trusted junior member of staff to go and get a vegetarian meal for the chief executive.

4. Approach the chief executive and explain what has happened and apologize on behalf of the catering company.

Your answer:

1. ____

2. ____

3. ____

4. ____

SITUATION 15

The only complaint I had about my job was that there was too much of it. I simply couldn't get everything done without stretching and stressing myself. Things got even worse with the recession. The company undertook a major cost-saving exercise and this meant even more for me to do and less support. I found it harder and harder to keep up with my workload and in the end I went to my doctor and he diagnosed stress-related illness. He signed me off work for a month.

Q15 Rate the suggested responses as: A. The most appropriate response; B. An acceptable response; C. A less than acceptable response.

The suggested responses:

1. Before I returned to work I would write to my manager informing him that my illness was stress-related and that I believed that it was caused by my workload and asking if my job to be changed so that the workload was more reasonable.

2. When I returned to work I would take care that I always took lunch breaks and left on time.

3. At the end of my period of sick leave I would go back to my doctor and seek a further period off work.

4. Before returning to work I would write to my manager to inform him that my stress-related illness was I believed caused by the amount of work I was expected to undertake and ask to meet him so that we might discuss ways in which my job might be reorganized so that the risk of my falling ill again was avoided.

Your answer:

1. ____
2. ____
3. ____
4. ____

Q16 If a stranger looked like he was lost I would volunteer to assist.

    A. Agree strongly

    B. Agree

    C. Do not agree or disagree

    D. Disagree

    E. Disagree strongly

Answer [_____]

Q17 If colleagues will not listen then it is sometimes necessary to raise your voice.

    A. Agree strongly

    B. Agree

    C. Do not agree or disagree

    D. Disagree

    E. Disagree strongly

Answer [_____]

SITUATION 18

Bereavement is something we all face at some stage or another. Even when it is expected after a long period of ill health it is still a terrible thing to have to deal with. When the person who dies is close to you then it affects everything. When it is your husband or wife then your private life is obviously turned upside down and how your friends and relatives relate to you is somehow different following the death. Going back to work after such bereavement often helps: it keeps you busy and helps make things seem more normal. At least that is what you thought but in your experience work soon became too much and you found it harder and harder to cope. In the end you felt you really needed to speak to your boss about how you felt and during the conversation you found that you could not hide your feeling any longer and you broke down in tears.

Q18 Rate the suggested responses as: A. The most appropriate response; B. An acceptable response; C. A less than acceptable response.

The suggested responses:

1. You would compose yourself as much as possible and continue with the conversation.

2. You would apologize and close the meeting.

3. You would compose yourself, ask your boss to make no allowances for your situation and as much as possible ensure everything at work is as it was before the bereavement.

4. You would take as much time as is required to compose yourself and then explore practical ways in which you workload might be adjusted to take your situation into account.

Your answer:

1. _____

2. _____

3. _____

4. _____

Q19 I prefer a working environment where everyone knows their role and responsibilities.

    A. Agree strongly

    B. Agree

    C. Do not agree or disagree

    D. Disagree

    E. Disagree strongly

Answer [   ]

Q20 I find it hard to cope when a series of things go wrong.

    A. Agree strongly

    B. Agree

    C. Do not agree or disagree

    D. Disagree

    E. Disagree strongly

Answer [   ]

Q21 A manager should plan for every eventuality.

    A. Agree strongly

    B. Agree

    C. Do not agree or disagree

    D. Disagree

    E. Disagree strongly

Answer [   ]

Q22 It is often best to tell people no more than is necessary.

    A. Agree strongly

    B. Agree

    C. Do not agree or disagree

    D. Disagree

    E. Disagree strongly

Answer [   ]

SITUATION 23

My manager often smells of alcohol and it appears she is drinking during the day, which makes me very uncomfortable. She often does not seem to know what is going on and makes bizarre requests and decisions. She takes a lot of time off work and this puts extra pressure on us all as we end up with a different temporary manager each time. I feel senior management have left us in a chaotic situation and it is unfair to us to have to work in this atmosphere. I am finding it a major source of upset.

Q23 Rate the suggested responses as: A. The most appropriate response; B. An acceptable response; C. A less than acceptable response.

The suggested responses:

1. I would go to HR and ask to speak to them anonymously about the situation.

2. She obviously has a major problem so I would just try to put up with it.

3. I would approach one of your HR representatives and share my concerns in as professional and empathetic manner as I could.

4. I would approach her directly and discuss with her my suspicions and the upset it is causing.

Your answer:

1. _____
2. _____
3. _____
4. _____

Q24 I dress quietly.

    A. Agree strongly

    B. Agree

    C. Do not agree or disagree

    D. Disagree

    E. Disagree strongly

Answer

Q25 I sometimes say foolish things.

    A. Agree strongly

    B. Agree

    C. Do not agree or disagree

    D. Disagree

    E. Disagree strongly

Answer

Q26 If a task is routine I tend to feel disheartened.

    A. Agree strongly

    B. Agree

    C. Do not agree or disagree

    D. Disagree

    E. Disagree strongly

Answer

SITUATION 27

One of the foremen at your place of work has a terrible reputation when it comes to how he treats his staff. He, for example, calls males 'boy', which the black members of his team say they find particularly offensive. He swears at all his team, using really objectionable terms of a sexual nature and which insult their mothers and sisters. Management know about it but they do nothing to stop it. You are so relieved that you do not work for him.

Q27 Rate the suggested responses as: A. The most appropriate response; B. An acceptable response; C. A less than acceptable response.

The suggested responses:

1. Support your colleagues by trying to work out with them what they can do about the harassment.

2. Tell friends what is going on.

3. Find out whether your employer has specific rules about harassment at work or a grievance procedure and encourage your colleagues to use them to raise the problem.

4. Offer to support your colleagues in an approach to your employer at first informally but if this does not work then through a formal grievance.

Your answer:

1. ____
2. ____
3. ____
4. ____

Q28 I can see a difficult job through to the end.

    A. Agree strongly

    B. Agree

    C. Do not agree or disagree

    D. Disagree

    E. Disagree strongly

Answer

Q29 It is important to question working practices.

    A. Agree strongly

    B. Agree

    C. Do not agree or disagree

    D. Disagree

    E. Disagree strongly

Answer

Q30 I can forgive, resolve differences and turn the page.

    A. Agree strongly

    B. Agree

    C. Do not agree or disagree

    D. Disagree

    E. Disagree strongly

Answer

SITUATION 31

It was the birthday of one of your crew and you agreed to meet at the pub at the end of the shift for a drink. There was the usual banter and jokes going on and it was all light-hearted and fun. However, you then heard someone tease Jane over her sexuality.

Q31 Rate the suggested responses as: A. The most appropriate response; B. An acceptable response; C. A less than acceptable response.

The suggested responses:

1. I would call the person who was teasing Jane an idiot and tell Jane to take no notice of the nonsense.

2. I would let Jane deal with it but explain to her afterwards that I witnessed the remark and if she needed me as a witness to make a formal complain at work the next day she need only ask.

3. If it had been in work then what was said would have contravened our code of conduct and I would have backed Jane in bringing a grievance against the person if that was what she had wished to do. However, it was outside work, so the code does not apply.

4. Harmless banter outside work is something we have to accept but if it upsets you then you should tell the person that it does and they should refrain from it in the future.

Your answer:

1. ____

2. ____

3. ____

4. ____

Q32 I most want to find out about the meaning of life.

    A. Agree strongly

    B. Agree

    C. Do not agree or disagree

    D. Disagree

    E. Disagree strongly

Answer [＿＿＿＿＿＿＿]

Q33 I keep problems to myself.

    A. Agree strongly

    B. Agree

    C. Do not agree or disagree

    D. Disagree

    E. Disagree strongly

Answer [＿＿＿＿＿＿＿]

Q34 I work best when I am in competition with others.

    A. Agree strongly

    B. Agree

    C. Do not agree or disagree

    D. Disagree

    E. Disagree strongly

Answer [＿＿＿＿＿＿＿]

SITUATION 35

You work for the regional airport and your employer is quarrying just beside the airport and crushing the recovered rock to form hardcore which is then used to expand the airport apron. The apron is where the jet planes stand when not in use. The airport gets really busy a couple of times a year and the extension of the apron must be finished in time for the next busy time. Key to the whole operation is a giant rock crusher. The crusher is being operated 24/7 to ensure that enough hardcore is produced in time. Your employer has asked if you would operate the crusher for a shift as the usual operator has asked to take a day off. You know the machine is potentially very dangerous.

Q35 Rate the suggested responses as: A. The most appropriate response; B. An acceptable response; C. A less than acceptable response.

The suggested responses:

1. I would ask the current operator to show me how to use the machine and once I felt I had got the hang of it I would work the shift.

2. I would operate the machine as asked because while the request is obviously dangerous only businesses employing five or more people must have plans in place to deal with any risks.

3. I would refuse to work the machine as it was not safe for me to do so and I would not worry about being threatened with disciplinary action because an employer can't make you do something unsafe.

4. I would explain that I was not suitably trained or experienced to work the rock crusher but if they could organize the necessary training I would be happy to operate it.

Your answer:

1. ____
2. ____
3. ____
4. ____

Q36 In work it is sometimes necessary to tell a little lie.

A. Agree strongly

B. Agree

C. Do not agree or disagree

D. Disagree

E. Disagree strongly

Answer [   ]

Q37 I prefer watching a sport such a golf or tennis than team sports.

A. Agree strongly

B. Agree

C. Do not agree or disagree

D. Disagree

E. Disagree strongly

Answer [   ]

Q38 I have a tendency to follow my own instincts rather than those of my manager.

A. Agree strongly

B. Agree

C. Do not agree or disagree

D. Disagree

E. Disagree strongly

Answer [   ]

SITUATION 39

Paul, like lots of people, believes that global warming threatens the existence of the human race. He spends a lot of his spare time visiting climate change websites and shares the latest views with the rest of the team. Some of your colleagues agree with him. Others either are not interested or respond negatively sometimes just to wind him up. However, he rarely talks about anything else and you all have become really fed up with his determination to convert you to his point of view. There have been a few stand-up rows and between you all you tried to agree a ban of all talk of climate change but Paul is as determined as he is dogmatic and he will not let the subject drop. As far as he is concerned whoever disagrees with him is a denier of the obvious facts.

Q39 Rate the suggested responses as: A. The most appropriate response; B. An acceptable response; C. A less than acceptable response.

The suggested responses:

1. I would take the matter up with my immediate manager and ask if he could intervene again and try to put a stop to the cause of the bad feeling.

2. I would suggest that we again all agree no more talk about climate change.

3. I would ask to be transferred to another watch.

4. I would go to the personnel officer and ask if there was anything they could do to help.

Your answer:

1. _____
2. _____
3. _____
4. _____

Q40 I prefer people who show their emotions.

    A. Agree strongly

    B. Agree

    C. Do not agree or disagree

    D. Disagree

    E. Disagree strongly

Answer [   ]

Q41 My work suffers if I'm interrupted when I'm trying to complete something complex.

    A. Agree strongly

    B. Agree

    C. Do not agree or disagree

    D. Disagree

    E. Disagree strongly

Answer [   ]

Q42 I would ask a colleague to sign off an important piece of work in case it later turns out to have faults.

    A. Agree strongly

    B. Agree

    C. Do not agree or disagree

    D. Disagree

    E. Disagree strongly

Answer [   ]

SITUATION 43

Your wife of 12 years has left you and most of your mutual friends found out when, even though you are still man and wife, she posted on Facebook that she is single and had moved out of the family home. She has stopped wearing her wedding ring and is fooling around with other men. As much as you try, your marriage problems are impacting on your work. Colleagues who had read the Facebook message naturally asked you what was happening, others have started to comment on the change in your approach at work and you know it is only a matter of time before your watch leader will ask you if everything is ok.

Q43 Rate the suggested responses as: A. The most appropriate response; B. An acceptable response; C. A less than acceptable response.

The suggested responses:

1. I would try even harder to ensure that my family problems do not impact on my job.

2. I would tell my co-workers and supervisor nothing; that way my personal problems can't affect my work.

3. I would tell my supervisor about my problems and ask him not to share them with anyone else and where practical to make allowances for the impact it was having on my work.

4. I would tell my co-workers and supervisor to please help me by keeping my private life separate from work.

Your answer:

1. ____

2. ____

3. ____

4. ____

Q44 There are some sorts of people I just know I'm not going to get on with.

   A. Agree strongly

   B. Agree

   C. Do not agree or disagree

   D. Disagree

   E. Disagree strongly

Answer [   ]

Q45 I would describe myself as happy-go-lucky.

   A. Agree strongly

   B. Agree

   C. Do not agree or disagree

   D. Disagree

   E. Disagree strongly

Answer [   ]

Q46 In my spare time I prefer to sit alone with a good book.

   A. Agree strongly

   B. Agree

   C. Do not agree or disagree

   D. Disagree

   E. Disagree strongly

Answer [   ]

SITUATION 47

You are entering the building where you work and find a man standing at the door. The door requires a pass to be placed over a pad before it opens and you use your pass to unlock the door. Without thinking you hold the door open for the person who enters with you and thanks you. He looks smart and businesslike but you do not recognize him. This does not mean that he does not work in the building or should not be inside as many people work there and you do not know them all. You decide to ask to see his security pass but he refuses and tells you that he works in security and that he does not have to show his pass.

Q47 Rate the suggested responses as: A. The most appropriate response; B. An acceptable response; C. A less than acceptable response.

The suggested responses:

1. Ask his name and go to your office and call security to check if it is true that he works there.

2. Politely insist that he shows you his pass.

3. Offer to accompany him to the office of the security team so that they may confirm he works there.

4. Let the matter drop.

Your answer:

1. ____

2. ____

3. ____

4. ____

Q48 My desk is more often than not a muddle.

    A. Agree strongly

    B. Agree

    C. Do not agree or disagree

    D. Disagree

    E. Disagree strongly

Answer [   ]

Q49 A policy of openness and giving people access to all the available information is the best.

    A. Agree strongly

    B. Agree

    C. Do not agree or disagree

    D. Disagree

    E. Disagree strongly

Answer [   ]

SITUATION 50

A colleague complains to you about the body odour of a member of your team. On a few occasions you have noticed the bad odour yourself but decided against saying anything as you are aware of some personal difficulties the individual faces.

Q50 Rate the suggested responses as: A. The most appropriate response; B. An acceptable response; C. A less than acceptable response.

The suggested responses:

1. You would quietly explain to your colleague the nature of the personal problems that the individual faces and ask them to be more understanding.

2. Resolve to raise the matter with the individual at the next team meeting and inform your colleague that you will handle it.

3. Ask your colleague to say no more on the subject and do nothing.

4. Meet privately with the member of your team and ask that they pay more attention to their personal hygiene.

Your answer:

1. ____

2. ____

3. ____

4. ____

Q51 I do not worry too much if a job is dangerous.

    A. Agree strongly

    B. Agree

    C. Do not agree or disagree

    D. Disagree

    E. Disagree strongly

Answer

Q52 A key quality of good leadership is the demonstration of integrity.

    A. Agree strongly

    B. Agree

    C. Do not agree or disagree

    D. Disagree

    E. Disagree strongly

Answer

Q53 I live by the rule that if you do me I will do you back.

    A. Agree strongly

    B. Agree

    C. Do not agree or disagree

    D. Disagree

    E. Disagree strongly

Answer

SITUATION 54

You overhear a heated conversation between two members of staff, neither of whom is in your team. You are shocked to hear one of the individuals threaten the other with physical violence. You know both the individuals concerned and can't really believe what you are hearing. Soon after the threat the individuals become aware of your presence and the conversation abruptly stops.

Q54 Rate the suggested responses as: A. The most appropriate response; B. An acceptable response; C. A less than acceptable response.

The suggested responses:

1. You would act as if you had heard nothing and not get involved.

2. You would take the matter up according to the procedure laid down in the staff handbook.

3. You would approach their respective line managers and report the matter to them.

4. You would speak to the two individuals and explain to them what you heard and that you consider it a very serious matter and something they need to sort out between themselves without resort to threats of violence.

Your answer:

1. ____
2. ____
3. ____
4. ____

Q55 It is better that a manager is partisan than objective in carrying out his duties.

A. Agree strongly

B. Agree

C. Do not agree or disagree

D. Disagree

E. Disagree strongly

Answer

Q56 I can sometimes be irresponsible.

A. Agree strongly

B. Agree

C. Do not agree or disagree

D. Disagree

E. Disagree strongly

Answer

Q57 If someone speaks slowly I can't help but feel frustration.

A. Agree strongly

B. Agree

C. Do not agree or disagree

D. Disagree

E. Disagree strongly

Answer

SITUATION 58

A visitor to your building reported that his mobile phone and packet of sweets went missing when he left a room he was using, to go to use the toilet facilities. There is a large sign in the room that states that personal belongings should not be left unattended and that the management could not take any responsibility for any loss or damage to personal items. The room is covered by a security camera and when you review the footage you observe a member of your staff enter the room and appear to pick up something from the table. You approach the member of staff and she confesses to taking the sweets but denies taking the mobile phone.

Q58 Rate the suggested responses as: A. The most appropriate response; B. An acceptable response; C. A less than acceptable response.

The suggested responses:

1. You would call the police and report the theft and tell them that you have CCTV footage which appears to identify the thief and that a member of staff has admitted to stealing one of the missing items.

2. You would insist that the individual replaces the sweets and apologizes to the visitor; you would also explain to the visitor that there was nothing you could do about the phone and remind her of the content of the sign in the room.

3. You would search the individual's desk and pockets to see if you could locate the phone.

4. You would arrange for a meeting between the visitor and the individual so that she could explain that she only took the sweets and apologize.

Your answer:

1. ____

2. ____

3. ____

4. ____

Q59 A lot of people think a joke or two is harmless fun but some people can't take them, so it is in fact unacceptable to joke around at work.

A. Agree strongly

B. Agree

C. Do not agree or disagree

D. Disagree

E. Disagree strongly

Answer [   ]

SITUATION 60

You are really excited about your first day in your dream post. You can't believe your luck in leading a national project of such importance and one that is so topical. You know that if you do well in this high-profile role your career could really take off. Your impression of the role is confirmed when a call from a reporter from a national newspaper is put through to you and you are asked to answer some questions and provide comments for an article that will appear in the paper the next morning.

Q60 Rate the suggested responses as: A. The most appropriate response; B. An acceptable response; C. A less than acceptable response.

The suggested responses:

1. You would ask the journalist for her telephone number and say that someone will phone her back once you have checked who is the most appropriate person to deal with her request.

2. You would explain that you are new in the post but are happy to provide comments provided that your name does not appear in the article.

3. You would answer the journalist's questions truthfully.

4. You would tell the journalist that you are new in the post and must check what the correct course of action is before you provide any comments.

Your answer:

1. ____
2. ____
3. ____
4. ____

SITUATION 61

You criticize a member of your staff for grammatical errors in a report and the individual denies being the author. You realize that you were mistaken but the individual concerned gets extremely angry and starts shouting and swearing.

Q61 Rate the suggested responses as: A. The most appropriate response; B. An acceptable response; C. A less than acceptable response.

The suggested responses:

1. You would interrupt them to instruct them to stop shouting and using bad language and you would tell them that when they have calmed down you wish to speak to them; you would then turn away and leave them.

2. You would let them have their say and then apologize and retract your criticism.

3. You would let them finish and calmly tell them not to shout and swear and then you would apologize and retract your criticism.

4. You would interrupt them to stop them and explain that you wish to apologize for your error but that it is entirely unacceptable for them to shout and use bad language and if they do not stop immediately you will walk away and discuss the matter with them later.

Your answer:

1. ____

2. ____

3. ____

4. ____

SITUATION 62

You find the role in which you are currently working very challenging because it is so boring. Initially you were enthusiastic about the new appointment but the role did not turn out to be what you expected and you feel that your development is being held back because you spend your time undertaking simple administrative tasks. In your opinion the role could be undertaken by an administrative officer and does not require someone like you in the grade of higher executive officer.

Q62 Rate the suggested responses as: A. The most appropriate response; B. An acceptable response; C. A less than acceptable response.

The suggested responses:

1. You would press on regardless and continue to do the best job that you could.

2. You would ask to meet your line manager and explain to her how you feel.

3. You would wait until your annual review and use that occasion to explain how you feel.

4. You would start looking for another job.

Your answer:

1. ＿＿＿

2. ＿＿＿

3. ＿＿＿

4. ＿＿＿

SITUATION 63

Your work requires you to travel extensively and you are expected to meet these costs from your own pocket and each month submit an expenses claim supported with paid invoices, receipts and tickets for each item. Early on in the month your appointment required you to stay overnight in a hotel and you have mislaid the hotel receipt. You have telephoned the hotel asking it to send you a duplicate invoice but it has not arrived in time for your claim. Your employer is very strict about expenses claims and you know that you will not be repaid without the receipt; you also know that it will not pay claims that are submitted late until the following month so there is no point in delaying your claim until the receipt arrives. The amount involved is a lot and you have already waited almost a month for it to be reimbursed.

Q63 Rate the suggested responses as: A. The most appropriate response; B. An acceptable response; C. A less than acceptable response.

The suggested responses:

1. Submit your claim without the hotel stay and claim it next month when the duplicate receipt has arrived.

2. Write a receipt up on your computer with the name of the hotel and the amount and submit it with your claim.

3. Approach your manager and explain what has happened and ask that you be paid the sum owed without the receipt.

4. Collect a load of receipts for items such as travel and meals out that do not relate to your work but are equal to the cost of the hotel stay and submit those instead.

Your answer:

1. ____   3. ____

2. ____   4. ____

SITUATION 64

Tomorrow is your first day as the manager of a project more complex than anything you have previously run. You have some concerns because the team has recently been criticized for poor record keeping. On the first day with your new team you need to start off on the right foot.

Q64 Rate the suggested responses as: A. The most appropriate response; B. An acceptable response; C. A less than acceptable response.

The suggested responses:

1. Start with an icebreaker exercise where you and each member of the team take turns to introduce themselves.

2. Meet the whole team and then meet each member of the team individually.

3. Start with a series of meetings one after the other with each member of the team and ask staff to bring their project files with them to the meeting so that you can go through them with them.

4. Spend the day alone reading all the background papers and files.

Your answer:

1. ____

2. ____

3. ____

4. ____

SITUATION 65

Your team provides a service seven days a week between the hours of 8am and 8pm. This is achieved by working one of two six-hour shifts; one starts at 8am, the other at 2pm. One of your staff approaches you to explain that her personal circumstances have changed and she would no longer be able to work at weekends until she has made alternative childcare arrangements.

Q65 Rate the suggested responses as: A. The most appropriate response; B. An acceptable response; C. A less than acceptable response.

The suggested responses:

1. You would call a meeting to discuss the person's change of personal circumstances and her request not to work weekends for a period.

2. You would ask her how long it will be before she can return to working weekends and if it is a reasonable length of time you would agree to her request.

3. You would try to organize things differently so that her change of circumstances can be accommodated.

4. You would explain that you must treat everyone equally and that therefore, like everyone else, she would have to continue to work weekends.

Your answer:

1. ____

2. ____

3. ____

4. ____

SITUATION 66

A member of your team complained of feeling stressed and apprehensive. You arranged to speak to him in private and he explained that he felt most apprehensive whenever anything went wrong at work and that he then feels helpless and unsure how he might help put things right.

Q66 Rate the suggested responses as: A. The most appropriate response; B. An acceptable response; C. A less than acceptable response.

The suggested responses:

1. You would explain his role and the extent of his responsibilities and explain how these fit in with the team overall; you would also say that he should come to speak to you at any time.

2. You would suggest that he goes to see his doctor.

3. You would ask him if there were any changes you could make that would help him feel less stressed and apprehensive.

4. You would tell him to snap out of it and pull himself together.

Your answer:

1. ____
2. ____
3. ____
4. ____

SITUATION 67

You are following the usual procedure to induct a new member of your team and are surprised to learn that she is dyslexic.

Q67 Rate the suggested responses as: A. The most appropriate response; B. An acceptable response; C. A less than acceptable response.

The suggested responses:

1. You would ask her if there were any special requirements that she needed to undertake her role and that should she need things organized differently you would do your best to accommodate her needs.

2. You would describe your commitment to equality of opportunity and how you believe in treating everyone the same.

3. You would explain that you are concerned that this will mean that you will have to provide her with a great deal of support.

4. You would ask her if this meant that she will not be able to undertake some tasks to the high standards expected of your department.

Your answer:

1. _____
2. _____
3. _____
4. _____

SITUATION 68

Part of your responsibilities includes the management of workers in the staff nursery school where there is currently a vacancy for a nursery nurse. You meet the nursery supervisor to sift applicants for the vacant position. One of the applicants is male and the supervisor explains that you should reject his application because she could not leave a male nursery nurse on his own with the children and he could not be allowed to change nappies on his own.

Q68 Rate the suggested responses as: A. The most appropriate response; B. An acceptable response; C. A less than acceptable response.

The suggested responses:

1. You would accept the supervisor's advice and reject the applicant.

2. You would suggest that you stop the sift and resume later after you have had a chance to re-read the nursery's policy documents and procedures.

3. You would point out that you would first like to obtain guidance from the human resources department that it is an appropriate thing to do in the circumstances.

4. You would refuse to reject the applicant, pointing out that if you did so it would be on the basis of gender, which you believe would be wrong.

Your answer:

1. ____
2. ____
3. ____
4. ____

SITUATION 69

Everyone in your team is from time to time late for work but one member is persistently late. In every other respect her performance is satisfactory. Her lateness usually amounts to no more than 15 minutes and she is happy to make up the lost time by staying late.

Every time you have a meeting with her to discuss her timekeeping she assures you that it will improve and normally it does but only for a few days before deteriorating and once again she starts arriving late for work.

Your organization requires that a member of the human resources team is informed of all matters relating to staff attendance and timekeeping.

Q69 Rate the suggested responses as: A. The most appropriate response; B. An acceptable response; C. A less than acceptable response.

The suggested responses:

1. Provided she continues to make up the time you would allow the lateness to continue.

2. You would suggest that she starts work 15 minutes later than everyone else and stays 15 minutes longer in the evening.

3. You would give her one last chance and explain that if the lateness does not stop you will alert the human resources team and then the matter will be out of your hands.

4. You would arrange a meeting with a representative of the human resources team to discuss the issue and you know they will issue a formal written warning advising the individual to improve her timekeeping or face further disciplinary action. If the lateness continues her employment will be terminated after a further two warnings.

Your answer:

1. ____   3. ____

2. ____   4. ____

SITUATION 70

You received a complaint regarding one of your staff who, with a colleague, attended a meeting as a representative of your company. The complaint was from an elected member of the local council and stated that your team member had implied that it was acceptable for a local councillor to lie. You were very surprised that the complaint was directed towards the particular member of staff because you could not imagine a more experienced and level-headed individual.

Q70 Rate the suggested responses as: A. The most appropriate response; B. An acceptable response; C. A less than acceptable response.

The suggested responses:

1. You would reply to the elected representative explaining that your member of staff could not have implied that it was acceptable for a councillor to lie and there must be some sort of misunderstanding.

2. You would immediately consult the individual concerned and ask if she recalled the incident that had given rise to the complaint. If she stated that she had not implied it was acceptable for a councillor to lie then you would write to the elected member providing your team member's version of events.

3. You would reply to the elected representative offering an unreserved apology for what must have been a misunderstanding because you know the person concerned to be an experienced level-headed individual.

4. You would interview both members of your team who attended the meeting and if they confirmed that no one had implied it was acceptable for a councillor to lie then you would write to the elected member explaining that you have investigated the complaint and you had found that no one had implied that lying was acceptable.

Your answer:

1. _____   2. _____   3. _____   4. _____

CHAPTER 6

Non-verbal assessments

I f you face the Ravens Matrices, the SHL induction reasoning tests (which is a fault diagnosis assessment), a spatial reasoning assessment, the UKCAT abstract reasoning paper or any other managerial or graduate non-verbal assessment then the practice in this chapter is for you. If you are one of the many candidates who look on these tests as awful or mind-numbing, if you consider them 'psycho-horrible' and wonder what the relevance is to performance in the job to which you have applied, then read on and get practising. You will soon get the better of your understandable anxiety and learn the techniques needed to do brilliantly in them.

This chapter offers well over 100 practice questions. The first 65 are ideal if you face an input-type or fault diagnosis sub-test. The remaining questions cover the main type of abstract reasoning tests and introduce three types of spatial reasoning test. Whichever type you face, the practice below will help you prepare. The answers and explanations are provided in Chapter 7. If you need more practice then you will find over 300 practice questions in the Kogan Page title, *How to Pass Diagrammatic Reasoning Tests*.

Fault diagnosis

These tests involve rules that must be applied to a sequence of shapes, numbers or letters. If you are applying for a technical job they will involve 'switches' that allow only certain changes to the sequence to occur. In the case of non-technical positions they are likely to involve symbols that change the figures, letters or objects that make up the sequence. For example, a symbol may signify that triangles must be replaced with squares, a code may reverse the letters and another may signify that a character must be dropped or added. All types require you to quickly visualize how the sequence will be transformed through a series of transformations and identify whether, and if so where, a fault in the application of the rules has occurred. Take the word 'quickly' seriously. Many candidates complain that there is insufficient time to attempt all the questions in this style of test. The highest scoring candidates are those who can maintain their accuracy while working quickly enough to attempt more questions than most other candidates.

There are two styles of question below. The first 15 detail each step in the transformation and it is your task to decide at which step an error occurred. The remaining questions only provide the opening sequence and the end result once the transformations have occurred.

Rules Q1–5

AB   Delete the last character

BC   Replace the third character with the next in the alphabet

CD   Insert the letter P between the third and fourth character

DE   Exchange the first and last character

EF   Replace the second character with the previous letter in the alphabet

FG   Replace the fifth character with the next in the alphabet

GH   Reverse the whole sequence of letters

HI   Delete the third character

Q1   MOZLUCK   → AB + FG + GH → (D)
                         ↓   ↓   ↓
                       (A) (B) (C)

(A) MOZLUC

(B) MOZLVC

(C) CVLZOM

(D) No fault

Answer [   ]

Q2   ULTIMATE   → HI + EF + CD → (D)
                         ↓   ↓   ↓
                       (A) (B) (C)

(A) ULIMATE

(B) UKIMATE

(C) UKPIMATE

(D) No fault

Answer [   ]

Q3 ILLUSTRATE → DE + GH + DE → (D)
↓ ↓ ↓
(A) (B) (C)

(A) ELLUSTRATI

(B) ETARTSULLI

(C) ITARTSULLE

(D) No fault

Answer

Q4 MEDITERRANEAN → AB + HI + EF → (D)
↓ ↓ ↓
(A) (B) (C)

(A) MEDITERRANEA

(B) MEITERRANEA

(C) MDDITERRANEA

(D) No fault

Answer

Q5 DESTINATION → GH + CD + GH → (D)
↓ ↓ ↓
(A) (B) (C)

(A) NOITANITSED

(B) NOIPTANITSED

(C) DESTINATPION

(D) No fault

Answer

Rules Q6–10

KL Switch the second and fifth characters

MN Replace the last character with the letter X

NO Insert the letters SA between the six and seventh characters

PQ Exchange the middle and last character

RS Switch the first and second characters

TU Replace the first letter with the letter B

VW Reverse the whole sequence of letters

XY Replace the middle character with the letter C

Q6 UVEFGKLQ $\rightarrow$ TU + KL + MN $\rightarrow$ (D)

$\quad\quad\quad\quad\quad\quad\quad\quad$ ↓$\quad$ ↓$\quad$ ↓

$\quad\quad\quad\quad\quad\quad\quad\quad$ (A)$\quad$ (B)$\quad$ (C)

(A) BKEFGKLQ

(B) BGKEFKKLQ

(C) BGKEFKKLX

(D) No fault

Answer

Q7 XYTHMTCGG $\rightarrow$ PQ + XY + NO $\rightarrow$ (D)

$\quad\quad\quad\quad\quad\quad\quad\quad$ ↓$\quad$ ↓$\quad$ ↓

$\quad\quad\quad\quad\quad\quad\quad\quad$ (A)$\quad$ (B)$\quad$ (C)

(A) XYTHGTCGM

(B) XYTHCTCGM

(C) XYTHLTCSAGM

(D) No fault

Answer

Q8 NHTEEINPP   → RS + VW + KL → (D)
                                ↓   ↓   ↓
                               (A)   (B)   (C)

(A) HNTEEINPP

(B) PPNIEETNH

(C) PINPEETNH

(D) No fault

Answer

Q9 TSTMTWNAS   → PQ + KL + XY → (D)
                                ↓   ↓   ↓
                               (A)   (B)   (C)

(A) TSTMSWNAT

(B) TTTMSWNAT

(C) TTTMCWNAT

(D) No fault

Answer

Q10 MMDIAATIC   → RS + MN + VW → (D)
                                ↓   ↓   ↓
                               (A)   (B)   (C)

(A) MMDIAATIC

(B) MMDIAATIX

(C) XITAAIDMM

(D) No fault

Answer

Rules Q11–15

AA Replace the third letter with the number 3

CC Replace the last letter with the previous one in the alphabet

GG Delete the third item in the sequence

II Replace the fifth letter with the number 7

KK Replace the first number with the letter Z

MM Replace the first letter with the number 9

OO Replace the fourth item with the letters WR

Q11 BA2W3KEVQ $\rightarrow$ AA + KK + OO $\rightarrow$ (D)

$\downarrow$ $\downarrow$ $\downarrow$

(A) (B) (C)

(A) BA33KEVQ

(B) BA23KEVQ

(C) BA2WRKEVQ

(D) No fault

Answer ▢

Q12 65LMMWE89 $\rightarrow$ CC + GG + MM $\rightarrow$ (D)

$\downarrow$ $\downarrow$ $\downarrow$

(A) (B) (C)

(A) 65LMMWD89

(B) 65MMWD89

(C) 65M9WD89

(D) No fault

Answer ▢

Q13 BF442B7CR $\quad \rightarrow$ II $+$ AA $+$ GG $\rightarrow$ (D)
$$\downarrow \quad \downarrow \quad \downarrow$$
$$\text{(A)} \quad \text{(B)} \quad \text{(C)}$$

(A) BF442B7C7

(B) BF44237CR

(C) BF4237CR

(D) No fault

Answer [   ]

Q14 BA97801SP $\quad \rightarrow$ KK $+$ OO $+$ II $\rightarrow$ (D)
$$\downarrow \quad \downarrow \quad \downarrow$$
$$\text{(A)} \quad \text{(B)} \quad \text{(C)}$$

(A) BNZ27801SP

(B) BNZWR801SP

(C) BNZR801SP

(D) No fault

Answer [   ]

Q15 SU$KUK999 $\quad \rightarrow$ AA $+$ GG $+$ MM $\rightarrow$ (D)
$$\downarrow \quad \downarrow \quad \downarrow$$
$$\text{(A)} \quad \text{(B)} \quad \text{(C)}$$

(A) SU$3UK999

(B) SU3UK999

(C) 9U3UK999

(D) No fault

Answer [   ]

Introduction to the remaining questions

In the remaining questions you are presented with the initial sequence and the output once all the changes have been made. It is your task to decide if a fault has occurred and if so at which step in the process it occurred.

The only faults that can occur relate to the way a code is implemented and if a fault has occurred there is only one in each question. So if the code states that the number 5 should replace a character and a number 6 appears in its place, the fault was with the code that stated a number 5 should replace the character. If the next code requires the character (which should have become the number 5) to then be moved and it is moved correctly, the error is with the initial code and not the move. So ignore the possibility that the character was correctly changed to a 5 in the first instance but was changed to a 6 when it was moved.

Rules

AB   Delete the first character

BC   Delete the last character

CD   Replace the second character with the number 2

DE   Replace the third character with the number 5

EF   Replace the second character with the previous letter in the alphabet

FG   Replace the fifth character with the next in the alphabet

GH   Reverse the whole sequence of letters

HI   Delete the third character

Q16 PRACTICE $\quad\quad\quad \rightarrow$ FG + AB + GH $\rightarrow$ ECIUCAR

$$\downarrow \quad\quad \downarrow \quad\quad \downarrow$$

$$\text{(A)} \quad\text{(B)} \quad\text{(C)}$$

(A)

(B)

(C)

(D) No fault

Answer

Q17 CHANNEL $\quad\quad\quad \rightarrow$ HI + EF + CD $\rightarrow$ C2ANNEL

$$\downarrow \quad\quad \downarrow \quad\quad \downarrow$$

$$\text{(A)} \quad\text{(B)} \quad\text{(C)}$$

(A)

(B)

(C)

(D) No fault

Answer

Q18 JOHNSON   → DE + GH + DE → NOSN5OJ

                      ↓   ↓   ↓

                  (A)   (B)   (C)

(A)

(B)

(C)

(D) No fault

Answer

Q19 GLOOMY   → CD + FG + HI → G2OLY

                      ↓   ↓   ↓

                  (A)   (B)   (C)

(A)

(B)

(C)

(D) No fault

Answer

Q20 CYCLONE   → BC + AB + EF → YBLON

                      ↓   ↓   ↓

                  (A)   (B)   (C)

(A)

(B)

(C)

(D) No fault

Answer

Rules

KL Switch the second and fifth characters

MN Replace the last character with the letter X

NO Insert the letters SA between the six and seventh characters

PQ Exchange the middle and last character

RS Switch the first and second characters

TU Replace the first letter with the letter B

VW Reverse the whole sequence of letters

XY Replace the middle character with the letter C

Q21 FACULTY   → KL + MN + XY → FLUCATX

                 ↓   ↓   ↓

                (A) (B) (C)

(A)

(B)

(C)

(D) No fault

Answer

Q22 RESIDENCE   → TU + KL + NO → BESIDESANCE

                 ↓   ↓   ↓

                (A) (B) (C)

(A)

(B)

(C)

(D) No fault

Answer

Q23 NAMBY-PAMBY   → XY + RS + VW → YBMAP-YBMAN
                     ↓   ↓   ↓
                   (A)   (B)   (C)

(A)

(B)

(C)

(D) No fault

Answer [   ]

Q24 SYMBOL   → RS + KL + TU → BOMBSL
                     ↓   ↓   ↓
                   (A)   (B)   (C)

(A)

(B)

(C)

(D) No fault

Answer [   ]

Q25 RATIONAL   → MN + NO + KL → ROTIANASAX
                     ↓   ↓   ↓
                   (A)   (B)   (C)

(A)

(B)

(C)

(D) No fault

Answer [   ]

Rules

AB   Delete the last character

BC   Replace the third character with the next in the alphabet

CD   Insert the letter P between the third and fourth character

DE   Delete the third character

EF   Change the fifth character to the number 8

FG   Change the middle character to the number 3

GH   Reverse the order of the first three characters

HI   Move the fifth character to the end of the sequence

Q26 DASHING   → FG + CD + AB → DASP3IN

                              ↓   ↓   ↓

                             (A) (B) (C)

(A)

(B)

(C)

(D) No fault

                              Answer [   ]

Q27 COMRADE   → BC + GH + HI → OOCRDEA

                              ↓   ↓   ↓

                             (A) (B) (C)

(A)

(B)

(C)

(D) No fault

                              Answer [   ]

Q28 BISCUIT   → BC + DE + AB → BICUIT
                       ↓   ↓   ↓
                      (A) (B) (C)

(A)

(B)

(C)

(D) No fault

Answer [   ]

Q29 ANIMATE   → FG + AB + HI → ANIAT3
                       ↓   ↓   ↓
                      (A) (B) (C)

(A)

(B)

(C)

(D) No fault

Answer [   ]

Q30 DISTANT   → EF + DE + CD → DISP8NT
                       ↓   ↓   ↓
                      (A) (B) (C)

(A)

(B)

(C)

(D) No fault

Answer [   ]

Rules

KL   Switch the second and fifth characters

MN   Move the last character in the sequence to the start

NO   Insert the letters SA between the six and seventh characters

PQ   Delete the middle character

RS   Switch the first and second characters

TU   Delete the first character

VW   Reverse the whole sequence of characters

XY   Add the number 4 to the end of the sequence

Q31 EXCLUSIVE   → KL + XY + TU → XULCSIVE4

                ↓   ↓   ↓

               (A) (B) (C)

(A)

(B)

(C)

(D) No fault

Answer

Q32 FLUTTER   → VW + RS + PQ → ERTTLF

                ↓   ↓   ↓

               (A) (B) (C)

(A)

(B)

(C)

(D) No fault

Answer

Q33 GRAMMER   → MN + NO + TU → RAMMESAR
                                  ↓   ↓   ↓
                              (A) (B) (C)

(A)

(B)

(C)

(D) No fault

                                    Answer [   ]

Q34 HELPFUL   → XY + RS + MN → 4EHLPFUL
                               ↓   ↓   ↓
                             (A) (B) (C)

(A)

(B)

(C)

(D) No fault

                                    Answer [   ]

Q35 INTELLIGENT   → PQ + KL + TU → ILTENLGENT
                               ↓   ↓   ↓
                             (A) (B) (C)

(A)

(B)

(C)

(D) No fault

                                    Answer [   ]

Rules

AB   Delete the first character

BC   Delete the last character

CD   Replace the second character with the number 4

DE   Replace the third character with the number 9

EF   Replace the third character with the previous letter in the alphabet

FG   Replace the fourth character with the next in the alphabet

GH   Reverse the whole sequence of letters

HI   Delete the fifth character

JK   Switch the first and last characters

LM   Switch the third and fourth characters

Q36 GIBBERISH   → AB + CD + EF → I4AERISH

                                 ↓   ↓   ↓

                             (A) (B) (C)

(A)

(B)

(C)

(D) No fault

Answer

Q37 HIGHLIGHT   → BC + DE + FG → HI9ILIGT

                                 ↓   ↓   ↓

                             (A) (B) (C)

(A)

(B)

(C)

(D) No fault

Answer

Q38 INCOGNITO   → GH + JK + HI → OTINOCNI
                    ↓   ↓   ↓
                 (A)   (B)   (C)

(A)

(B)

(C)

(D) No fault

Answer [　　　　　　]

Q39 JOURNALIST   → AB + LM + BC → OUNRALIST
                    ↓   ↓   ↓
                 (A)   (B)   (C)

(A)

(B)

(C)

(D) No fault

Answer [　　　　　　]

Q40 LEISURE   → GH + HI + GH → LEISRE
                    ↓   ↓   ↓
                 (A)   (B)   (C)

(A)

(B)

(C)

(D) No fault

Answer [　　　　　　]

Rules

KL Switch the third and sixth characters

MN Move the second from last character in the sequence to the start

NO Insert the letter Z between the fifth and sixth characters

PQ Delete the first character

RS Switch the first and second characters

TU Delete the last character

VW Reverse the whole sequence of characters

XY Add the number 4 to the end of the sequence

Q41 OUTLINE   → XY + TU + PQ → OUTLINE

                                ↓   ↓   ↓

                            (A)   (B)   (C)

(A)

(B)

(C)

(D) No fault

Answer [　　　　　　]

Q42 MAINENANCE   → MN + VW + RS → NEANENAIMC

                                ↓   ↓   ↓

                            (A)   (B)   (C)

(A)

(B)

(C)

(D) No fault

Answer [　　　　　　]

Q43 NARCOTIC   → NO + KL + XY → NAZCORTIC4
$\qquad\qquad\qquad$ ↓ $\quad$ ↓ $\quad$ ↓
$\qquad\qquad\qquad$ (A) $\quad$ (B) $\quad$ (C)

(A)

(B)

(C)

(D) No fault

$\qquad\qquad\qquad\qquad\qquad$ Answer ☐

Q44 REFEREE   → VW + TU + RS → EEREFER
$\qquad\qquad\qquad$ ↓ $\quad$ ↓ $\quad$ ↓
$\qquad\qquad\qquad$ (A) $\quad$ (B) $\quad$ (C)

(A)

(B)

(C)

(D) No fault

$\qquad\qquad\qquad\qquad\qquad$ Answer ☐

Q45 PERIOD   → VW + NO + VW → DOIREZP
$\qquad\qquad\qquad$ ↓ $\quad$ ↓ $\quad$ ↓
$\qquad\qquad\qquad$ (A) $\quad$ (B) $\quad$ (C)

(A)

(B)

(C)

(D) No fault

$\qquad\qquad\qquad\qquad\qquad$ Answer ☐

Codes

— Replace the second shape with ▲

▲ Change all circles to unshaded squares

☐ Place the shape ■ between the second and third items in the sequence

△ Replace all shaded shapes with unshaded triangles (with apex at the top)

▼ Add a ▲ between the third and fourth shape

○ Replace the first shape with a shaded triangle with its apex pointing downwards

● Change the middle shape to an unshaded circle

Q46 ▲ △▼○   → —   + + ○   → ▲▲○▼○
                         ↓   ↓   ↓
                        (A)   (B)   (C)

(A)

(B)

(C)

(D) No fault

Answer [   ]

Q47 ● ● ○ —   → ▲ + ▼ + ○   → ▼☐▼—
                         ↓   ↓   ↓
                        (A)   (B)   (C)

(A)

(B)

(C)

(D) No fault

Answer [   ]

Q48 ▬ ▬ ○ ▬   → ▲ + ○ + ▬ → ▼▲■▬
                      ↓   ↓   ↓
                     (A)   (B)   (C)

(A)

(B)

(C)

(D) No fault

Answer

Q49 ○ ○ ● ○   → ▲ + ▼ + ○ → ▼□▲□□
                      ↓   ↓   ↓
                     (A)   (B)   (C)

(A)

(B)

(C)

(D) No fault

Answer

Q50 □ ○ □ ○   → □ + ● + ▲ → □○○▲□○
                      ↓   ↓   ↓
                     (A)   (B)   (C)

(A)

(B)

(C)

(D) No fault

Answer

Codes

♫   Remove all shading

@   Switch first and second shape

Σ   Add a □ to the end of series

Ω   Replace the first shape with ▲

╫   Shade the last shape

£   Replace the middle shape with ■

®   Switch the third and last shape

Q51 ○ ● ■ □   → ♫ + Σ + £   → ○ ○ □ □ □

                            ↓   ↓   ↓

                          (A)   (B)   (C)

(A)

(B)

(C)

(D) No fault

                               Answer

Q52 ▲ ▼ ○ ●   → ® + ╫ + @   → ▼ ▲ ● ○

                            ↓   ↓   ↓

                          (A)   (B)   (C)

(A)

(B)

(C)

(D) No fault

                               Answer

Q53 ●□●□   → ♬ + ╫ + Ω → ○□○■
                    ↓   ↓   ↓
                   (A) (B) (C)

(A)

(B)

(C)

(D) No fault

Answer [   ]

Q54 ▲▲▲△   → ® + Σ + £ → ▲▲■▲□
                    ↓   ↓   ↓
                   (A) (B) (C)

(A)

(B)

(C)

(D) No fault

Answer [   ]

Q55 □○□○   → Ω + @ + ♬ → ○Δ□○
                    ↓   ↓   ↓
                   (A) (B) (C)

(A)

(B)

(C)

(D) No fault

Answer [   ]

Codes

■□	Replace all shaded triangles with unshaded squares
●○	Reverse the order of all shapes in the sequence
▲▶	Shade all the shapes if they are not already shaded
▼◀	Exchange the first and last shape
□△	Reverse the shading of all shapes
▬▌	Insert a ▲ after the third shape
□▲	Replace all unshaded circles with shaded triangles
▌▬	Delete every other shape

Q56 ▲ ○ □ ●   → ■□ + ●○ + ▼◀ → ● □ ○ □

                              ↓   ↓   ↓
                            (A)   (B)   (C)

(A)

(B)

(C)

(D) No fault

Answer [ ]

Q57 △ ● ■ □   → □△ + ■□ + ▌▬ → ▲ □

                              ↓   ↓   ↓
                            (A)   (B)   (C)

(A)

(B)

(C)

(D) No fault

Answer [ ]

Q58 □■□■□   → ▌— + ▲▶ + —▌ → ■■■▲
↓ ↓ ↓
(A) (B) (C)

(A)

(B)

(C)

(D) No fault

Answer

Q59 ■□▲△   → —▌ + ▼◀ + ●○ → ■△▲□△
↓ ↓ ↓
(A) (B) (C)

(A)

(B)

(C)

(D) No fault

Answer

Q60 ○○▲▲   → □△ + ■□ + ▌— → □□□
↓ ↓ ↓
(A) (B) (C)

(A)

(B)

(C)

(D) No fault

Answer

Codes

- ● Exchange the fourth characters between the TWO sequences
- ☐ Reverse the TOP sequence
- ■ Insert the letter N after the second character in the LOWER sequence
- Δ Reverse the LOWER sequence
- ▼ Exchange the fifth characters between the TWO sequences
- ○ Exchange the second and fourth characters in the LOWER sequence
- ▲ Insert the letter L after the fifth character in the TOP sequence

Q61 GRECKLE   → ● + ■ + ▼ → GREAKLE
OXYACID   ↓   ↓   ↓   OXNYCCID
              (A) (B) (C)

(A)

(B)

(C)

(D) No fault

Answer [   ]

Q62 DECKCHAIR   → ▲ + ▼ + ■ → DECKMHAIR
PALOMINO   ↓   ↓   ↓   PANLOCLINO
              (A) (B) (C)

(A)

(B)

(C)

(D) No fault

Answer [   ]

Q63 BOUNCER   → □ + Δ + ○ → RECNUOB
       PORTRAIT   ↓   ↓   ↓   TRAITROP
                 (A)   (B)   (C)

(A)

(B)

(C)

(D) No fault

                            Answer [   ]

Q64 GADZOOK   → ● + Δ + ▲ → GADZOLOK
       LANOLIN   ↓   ↓   ↓   NILONAL
                 (A)   (B)   (C)

(A)

(B)

(C)

(D) No fault

                            Answer [   ]

Q65 MARAUD   → □ + ▼ + ○ → DUARNM
       SPLENDID   ↓   ↓   ↓   SELPADID
                 (A)   (B)   (C)

(A)

(B)

(C)

(D) No fault

                            Answer [   ]

Abstract reasoning

You will face abstract or inductive reasoning assessments for a great many positions. They often feature in the battery of tests used to select for managerial positions, graduate trainee programmes, students for medical schools, air traffic controllers and architects to give but a few examples. In fact you may well face one for any position where you need to think conceptually and analytically and indentify abstract patterns and trends.

The practice below will help you face the vast majority of styles of abstract reasoning tests. They all involve a series of pictorial or diagrammatic questions with little or no resort to words or numbers. The four principal sorts are covered: those that require you to identify a quality that is common; correctly complete a series; identify the correct code; and correctly identify the group to which the question shape belongs.

You can improve your likely score in every sort of abstract reasoning test. Whatever the particular task the practice below will ensure you become familiar with the key principles and competencies examined. The main ones are identifying patterns involving rotation, alteration, substitution, consistency and attention to detail of, for example, the number, size, shape, shading direction or location relative to other shapes.

Use the following 55 questions to become faster and more confident and accurate in every sort of abstract reasoning test. You will find over 100 more abstract practice questions in *How to Pass Diagrammatic Reasoning Tests*, published by Kogan Page.

Identify a quality in common

In the first type of abstract question you are presented with two question shapes and three suggested answers. Your task is to identify the feature that the two question shapes have in common and which one of the suggested answers also shares that quality.

Q1   Question shapes

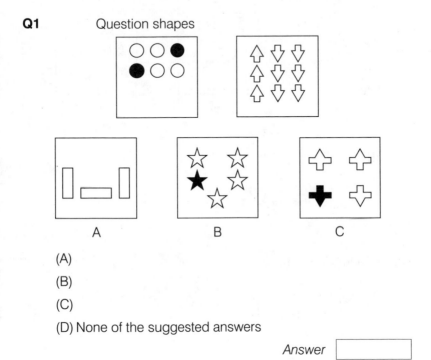

(A)

(B)

(C)

(D) None of the suggested answers

Answer

Q2   Question shapes

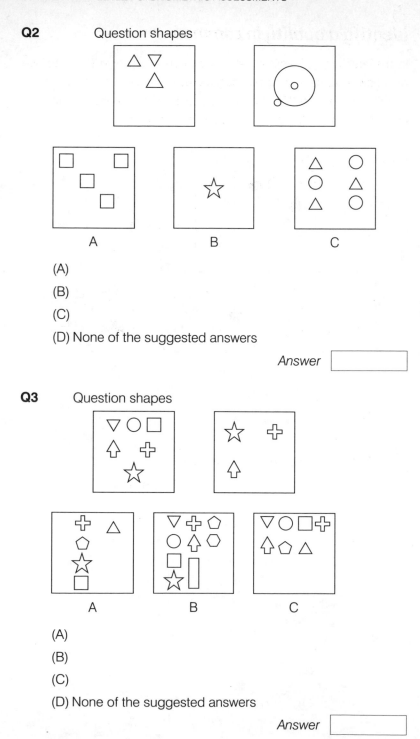

(A)

(B)

(C)

(D) None of the suggested answers

Answer

Q3   Question shapes

(A)

(B)

(C)

(D) None of the suggested answers

Answer

Q4 Question shapes

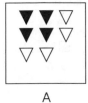 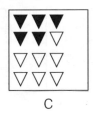

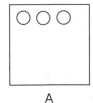

A   B   C

(A)

(B)

(C)

(D) None of the suggested answers

Answer

Q5 Question shapes

  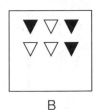

A   B   C

(A)

(B)

(C)

(D) None of the suggested answers

Answer

Q6   Question shapes

(A)

(B)

(C)

(D) None of the suggested answers

Answer [   ]

Q7   Question shapes

(A)

(B)

(C)

(D) None of the suggested answers

Answer [   ]

Q8   Question shapes

 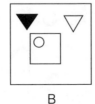 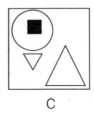

A   B   C

(A)

(B)

(C)

(D) None of the suggested answers

Answer

Q9   Question shapes

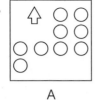 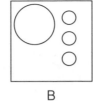 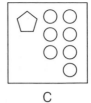

A   B   C

(A)

(B)

(C)

(D) None of the suggested answers

Answer

Q10   Question shapes

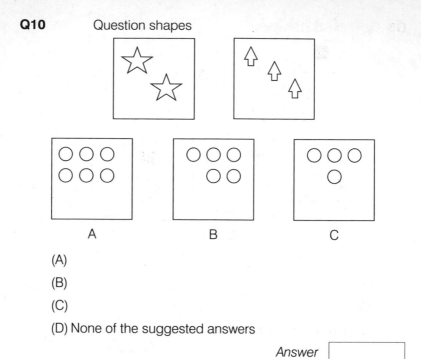

(A)

(B)

(C)

(D) None of the suggested answers

Answer

Complete a series

This, the second style of abstract reasoning question, requires you to complete a series or sequence of shapes by identifying which of the suggested answers should be placed in the empty space. Once again these questions test your ability to recognize sequences that maybe involve a principle of maths: rotation – where a shape is turned; alteration – where a shape changes into something else and is in some cases then changed back; consistency – where a change is made to a shape and is then consistently applied; replacement – where a shape or shapes is or are replaced by others; and attention to detail – where you simply have to look carefully at the diagrams.

Q11

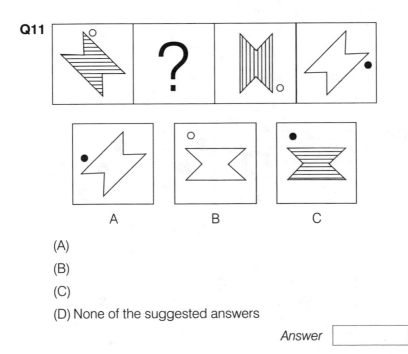

(A)

(B)

(C)

(D) None of the suggested answers

Answer

Q12

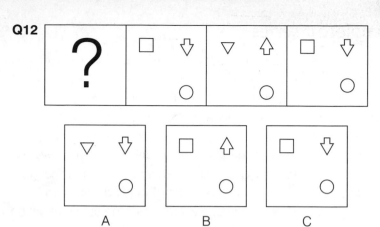

(A)

(B)

(C)

(D) None of the suggested answers

Answer

Q13

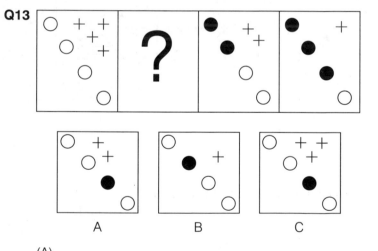

(A)

(B)

(C)

(D) None of the suggested answers

Answer

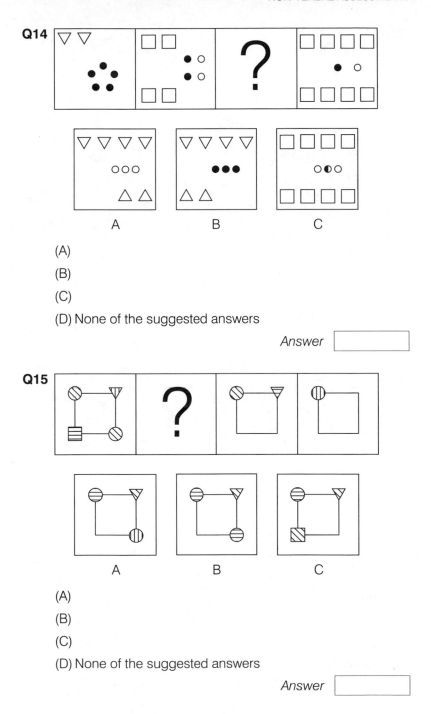

Q14

A

B

C

(A)

(B)

(C)

(D) None of the suggested answers

Answer

Q15

A

B

C

(A)

(B)

(C)

(D) None of the suggested answers

Answer

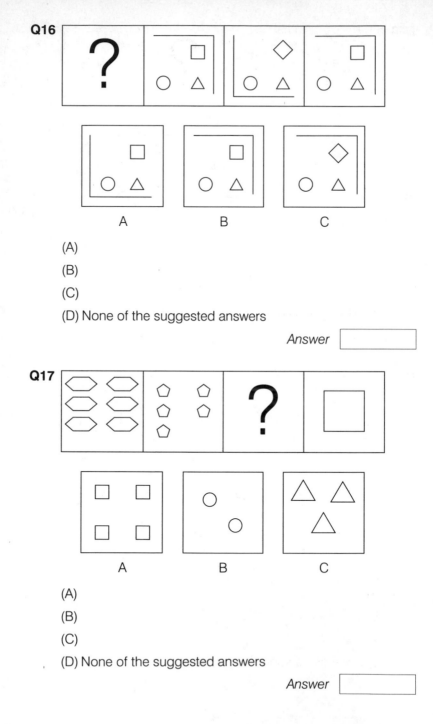

Q16

(A)

(B)

(C)

(D) None of the suggested answers

Answer

Q17

(A)

(B)

(C)

(D) None of the suggested answers

Answer

Q18

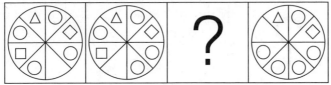

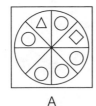 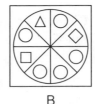 

A   B   C

(A)

(B)

(C)

(D) None of the suggested answers

Answer [   ]

Q19

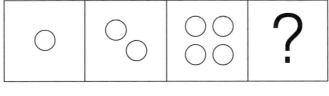

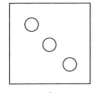 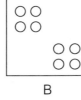 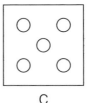

A   B   C

(A)

(B)

(C)

(D) None of the suggested answers

Answer [   ]

Q20

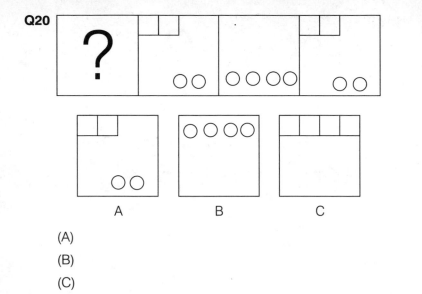

(A)

(B)

(C)

(D) None of the suggested answers

Answer

Identify the correct code

In this the fourth style of question your task is to identify the correct code for a new shape from the codes given for example shapes. Note that in some instances your answer is restricted to choosing from the suggested answers.

Q21 Choose from the suggested codes the one most suitable for the question shape.

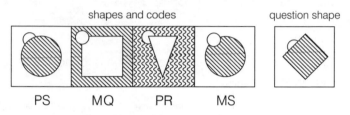

| shapes and codes | question shape |

PS   MQ   PR   MS

Suggested answers: MR, MS, PS

Answer ☐

Q22 Choose from the suggested codes the one most suitable for the question shape.

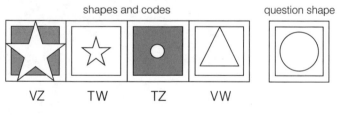

| shapes and codes | question shape |

VZ   TW   TZ   VW

Suggested answers: VW, TW, VZ

Answer ☐

Q23 Choose from the suggested codes the one most suitable for the question shape.

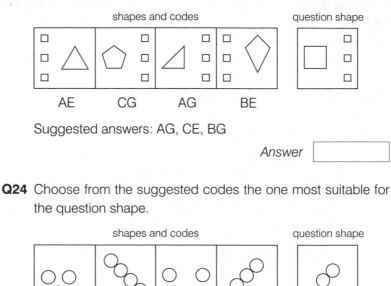

Suggested answers: AG, CE, BG

Answer

Q24 Choose from the suggested codes the one most suitable for the question shape.

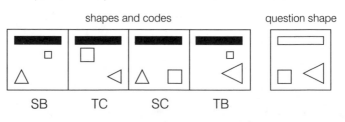

Suggested answers: PK, NG, NK

Answer

Q25 Choose from the suggested codes the one most suitable for the question shape.

shapes and codes   question shape

SB   TC   SC   TB

Suggested answers: TC, TB, SC

Answer

Q26 Write the code for the question shape in the answer box.

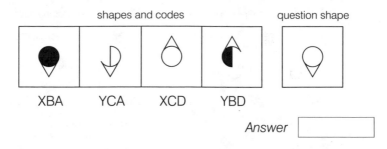

shapes and codes   question shape

XBA   YCA   XCD   YBD

Answer

Q27 Write the code for the question shape in the answer box.

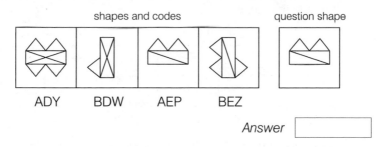

shapes and codes   question shape

ADY   BDW   AEP   BEZ

Answer

Q28 Write the code for the question shape in the answer box.

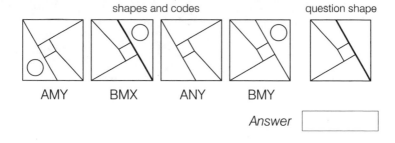

shapes and codes   question shape

AMY   BMX   ANY   BMY

Answer

Q29 Write the code for the question shape in the answer box.

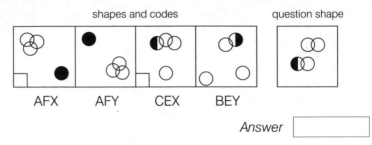

Answer [   ]

Q30 Choose from the suggested code the one most suitable for the question shape.

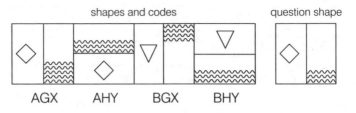

Suggested answers: BGY, AHX, AHY

Answer [   ]

Allocate the three question shapes to the correct set

In this style of test your task is to allocate the three question shapes to sets of shapes or to conclude that the question shape belongs to neither set. Each of the two sets comprises three shapes and you must first identify a pattern in the set and decide which if any of the question shapes follows the same pattern. Each question requires you to provide three answers. For example, you might decide the question shape 1 belongs to set A, Question shape 2 to neither and Question shape 3 to set B. It is possible for more than one question shape to be allocated to a set.

Q31

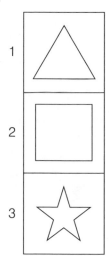

Set A   Set B

Answer (N = neither set A nor B)

	A	B	N
1			
2			
3			

Q32

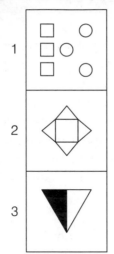

Set A   Set B

Answer (N= neither set A nor B)

	A	B	N
1			
2			
3			

Q33

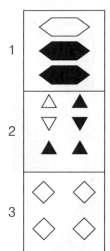

Set A   Set B

Answer (N = neither set A nor B)

	A	B	N
1			
2			
3			

Q34

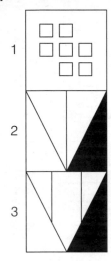

Set A   Set B

Answer (N = neither set A nor B)

	A	B	N
1			
2			
3			

Q35

Set A   Set B

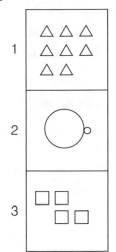

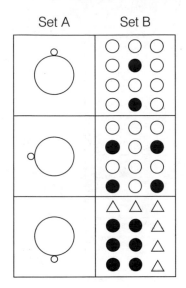

Answer (N = neither set A nor B)

	A	B	N
1			
2			
3			

Q36

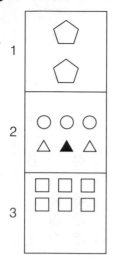

Answer (N = neither set A nor B)

	A	B	N
1			
2			
3			

Q37

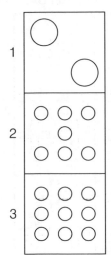

Set A   Set B

Answer (N = neither set A nor B)

	A	B	N
1			
2			
3			

Q38

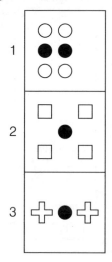

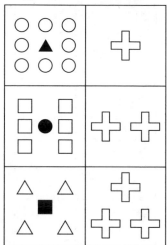

Answer (N = neither set A nor B)

	A	B	N
1			
2			
3			

Q39

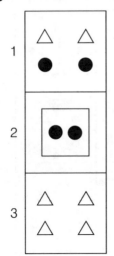

Set A   Set B

Answer (N = neither set A nor B)

	A	B	N
1			
2			
3			

Q40

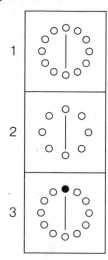

Set A   Set B

Answer (N = neither set A nor B)

	A	B	N
1			
2			
3			

Spatial recognition and visual estimation

Below you will find practice for three types of spatial or visual estimation tests. In the first example your task is to identify the plan of a three-dimensional shape. A plan is the view of the shape if you were looking exactly down on it. In the second type you have to identify the shape that has been rotated but is otherwise identical to the question shape (all the others would have been rotated but changed in some way too). In the last type of question you must identify the shape that could be contrasted if the two example shapes are combined. No change should be made to the shapes other than combining them.

You will find 100 practice questions for spatial recognition and visual estimation in *How to Pass Diagrammatic Reasoning Tests*, published by Kogan Page. You will also find hundreds of practice questions for input type and abstract diagrammatic reasoning sub-tests.

Type 1. Identify the plan of the three-dimensional shape

Q41

A

B

C

Answer

Q42

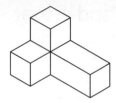

A

B

C

Answer

Q43

A

B

C

Answer

Q44

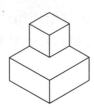

A

B

C

Answer

Q45

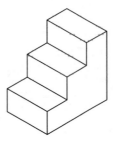

A

B

C

Answer

Type 2. Identify the shape that has been rotated but is otherwise identical to the question shape

Q46

A

B

C

D

Answer

Q47

A   B

C 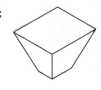   D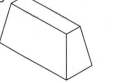

Answer

Q48

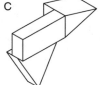

A 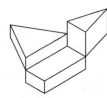   B

C 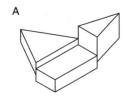   D

Answer

Q49

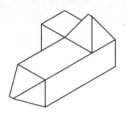

A

B

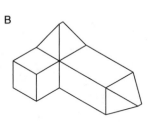

C

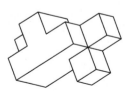

Answer

Q50

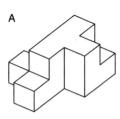

A

B

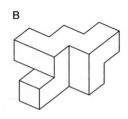

C

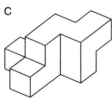

Answer

Type 3. Identify the new shape that could be constructed if the two example shapes were combined

Q51

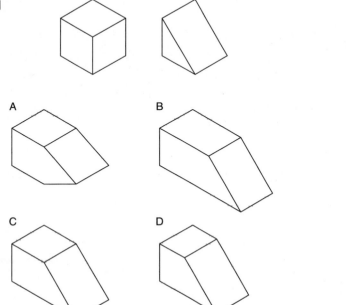

A

B

C

D

Answer

Q52

A

B

C

D

Answer

Q53

A

B

C

D

Answer

Q54

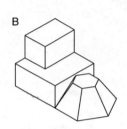

A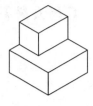

B

C

Answer

Q55

A

B

C

Answer

CHAPTER 7

Answers and detailed explanations

Chapter 3. Numerical assessments

Quantitative reasoning

Practice start 1

Q1 *Answer:* A, 20% loss
Explanation: 40 − 32 = 8 loss, 8 ÷ 40 = 0.2 × 100 = 20

Q2 *Answer:* C, 60% profit
Explanation: 0.80 − 0.50 = 0.30 profit, 0.30 ÷ 0.50 = 0.6 × 100 = 60

Q3 *Answer:* B, 25% profit
Explanation: 5 − 4 = 1 profit, 1 ÷ 4 = 0.25 × 100 = 25

Q4 *Answer:* C, 12.5% loss
Explanation: 8 − 7 = 1 loss, 1 ÷ 8 = 0.125 × 100 = 12.5

Q5 *Answer:* A, 18% loss
Explanation: 290 − 237.78 = 52.2 ÷ 290 = 0.18 × 100 = 18

Q6 *Answer:* D, 23% loss
Explanation: 82 − 63.14 = 18.86 loss, 18.86 ÷ 82 = 0.23 × 100
= 23

Q7 *Answer:* B, 25% profit
Explanation: 25 − 20 = 5 profit, 5 ÷ 20 = 0.25 × 100 = 25

Q8 *Answer:* D, 3% loss
Explanation: 370 − 358.90 = 11.1 loss, 11.1 ÷ 370 =
0.03 × 100 = 3

Q9 *Answer:* A, 32% profit
Explanation: 660 − 500 = 160 profit, 160 ÷ 500 =
0.32 × 100 = 32

Q10 *Answer:* 80% loss
Explanation: 12 − 2.4 = 9.6 loss, 9.6 ÷ 12 = 0.8 × 100 = 80

Currency conversions

Practice start 2

Q1 *Answer:* T$75
Explanation: 50 × 1.5 = 75

Q2 *Answer:* T$52.5
Explanation: 1.75 × 30 = 52.2

Q3 *Answer:* T$112
Explanation: 1.4 × 80 = 112

Q4 *Answer:* T$22.5
Explanation: 0.9 × 25 = 22.5

Q5 *Answer:* T$37.5
Explanation: 0.15 × 250 = 37.5

Q6 *Answer:* EC$5
Explanation: 20 ÷ 4 = 5

Q7 *Answer:* EC$16
Explanation: 40 ÷ 2.5 = 16

Q8 *Answer:* EC$2
Explanation: 2.5 ÷ 1.25 = 2

Q9   *Answer:* EC$4
       Explanation: $7 \div 1.75 = 4$

Q10 *Answer:* EC$40
       Explanation: $60 \div 1.5 = 40$

Practice start 3

Q1   *Answer:* HC$8
       Explanation: $20 \div 2.5 = 8$

Q2   *Answer:* HC$5
       Explanation: $9 \div 1.8 = 5$

Q3   *Answer:* HC$4
       Explanation: $18 \div 4.5 = 4$

Q4   *Answer:* HC$5
       Explanation: $8 \div 1.6 = 5$

Q5   *Answer:* HC$50
       Explanation: $55 \div 1.1 = 50$

Q6   *Answer:* EC$5
       Explanation: EC$1 = T$2 so T$10 = $(10 \div 2) = 5$

Q7   *Answer:* EC$0.25
       Explanation: $1.5 \div 6 = EC0.25$

Q8   *Answer:* EC$15
       Explanation: $48 \div 3.2 = 15$

Q9   *Answer:* EC$6.5
       Explanation: EC$1 = T$4 so T$26 = $(26 \div 4) = 6.5$

Q10 *Answer:* EC$8
       Explanation: EC$1 = T$3 so T$24 = $(24 \div 3) = 8$

Practice start 4

Q1   *Answer:* EC$5
       Explanation: $3.6 \div 3 = 1.2$ so EC$1 = T$1.2 and
       T$6 = $(6 \div 1.2) = EC\$5$

Q2   *Answer:* EC$12
       Explanation: EC$2 = T$2.5 so T$15 = $(15 \div 2.5) =$
       EC$6 $\times$ 2 = EC$12

Q3 *Answer:* EC$12

Explanation: T$1 = EC9.5 so T$114 = (114 ÷ 9.5) = EC$12

Q4 *Answer:* EC$4

Explanation: notice that 7 is twice 3.5 so double EC$2 to get the answer otherwise EC$1 = T$1.75 so T$7 = (7 ÷ 1.75) = EC$4

Q5 *Answer:* EC$11

Explanation: EC$1 = T$2 so T$22 = (22 ÷ 2) = 11

Q6 *Answer:* EC$6

Explanation: EC$1 = T$3 so T$18 = (18 ÷ 3) = EC$6

Q7 *Answer:* EC$4

Explanation: EC$1 = (2.25 ÷ 3) = 0.75 so T$3 = (3 × 0.75) = 4

Q8 *Answer:* EC$18

Explanation: T$1 is worth EC$2 so T$9 = EC$18

Q9 *Answer:* EC$5

Explanation: EC$1 = (6.6 ÷ 3) = T$2.2 so T$11 = (11 ÷ 2.2) = 5

Q10 *Answer:* EC$285.7

Explanation: EC$1 = (1.4 ÷ 4) = 0.35 so T$100 = EC$285.7

Data sufficiency

Practice start 5

Q1 *Answer:* B

Explanation: An equilateral triangle has three equal sides and equal angles so the statement can be answered with B alone. Statement 1 may be true but you cannot tell from it alone and as you can answer it with statement 2 you do not need both 1 and 2 to answer it.

Q2 *Answer:* False

Explanation: The answer to the quadratic $y^2 - y - 2 = 0$ is both 2 and −1 so it is false to say that y is negative as it can also be the positive number 2.

Q3 *Answer:* C

Explanation: statement 1 is true of squares and rectangles, statement 2 is true of both squares and rhombus but both are true only of squares.

Q4 *Answer:* True

Explanation: $4^3 = 64$ and $8^2 = 64$

Q5 *Answer:* C

Explanation: The area of the isosceles triangle can be established if its height can be calculated. And with 1 and 2 together we can calculate its height and so its area by dividing the isosceles triangle into two right-angled triangles, then calculating the height of the isosceles triangle using Pythagoras. Once the height is established then the area can be calculated.

Q6 *Answer:* False

Explanation: To find the sum you must find the average. The average is $20 + 48 = 68 \div 2 = 34$, sum $= 29 \times 34 = 986$. 29 is the number of items in the range $48 - 20 = 28 + 1 = 29$. You have to add 1 otherwise you miscount the items, which is the error made in the question.

Q7 *Answer:* D

Explanation: Statement 1 proves the triangle is an equilateral so not right-angled; statement 2 can be used to test the given lengths using Pythagoras' theorem. In this case the lengths are a Pythagoras triple and multiples of any triple are also right-angled.

Q8 *Answer:* True

Explanation: There are 36 possible outcomes and 4 successful outcomes (ie 4 combinations that have a sum of 5) and $4/36 = 1/9$.

Q9 *Answer:* D

Explanation: All five-sided shapes are pentagons so the two statements are the same. Either statement is sufficient to answer the question because for any polygon you can establish the number of triangles into which it can be divided with the formula, number of sides $- 2 =$ number of triangles.

Q10 *Answer:* True

Explanation: 7 + 3 + 9 = 19; 399,000 ÷ 19 = 21,000; lowest payout is 3 × 21,000 = 63,000; highest payout is 9 × 21,000 = 189,000, difference = 126,000.

Practice start 6

Q1 *Answer:* D

Explanation: An integer is a whole number. Statement 1 means that (n + 8)/8 is an integer, so n/8 + 8 is an integer, therefore n must be divisible with no remainder. Statement 2 would give a similar result. Either statement is sufficient.

Q2 *Answer:* Cannot tell

Explanation: We cannot calculate the area of a triangle without first establishing its height and we cannot do that with the information provided.

Q3 *Answer:* A

Explanation: The cost of the similar bar can be calculated from statement 1 as a corresponding ratio. No comparison can be drawn from statement, 2 however, so it alone or with 1 is insufficient.

Q4 *Answer:* True

Explanation: A parallelogram has two pairs of opposite sides that are parallel so the diagonals divide it into two equal parts (in other words bisect it).

Q5 *Answer:* C

Explanation: To calculate by how much the water will rise we must establish the volume of the ball bearing and the area of the base of the beaker. To do this we require the information provided in both statements. Google 'area of a circle' and 'volume of a sphere' if you need to review these formulas.

Q6 *Answer:* True

Explanation: Let the sides = 10 giving an area of 10^2 = 100. Now increase the length of the sides to 13 (10 × 130%) which gives an area of 13^2 = 169. The area has increased from 100 to 169, an increase of 69%.

Q7 *Answer:* E

Explanation: To complete the calculation we need to know that the ground is level and either the length of the ladder or its distance along the ground from the wall, but we do not know this so the data is insufficient.

Q8 *Answer:* True

Explanation: A pentagon has five sides, five interior angles and the sum of the interior angles = 540°. Therefore the size of the remaining four angles can be calculated to be 110° (note it is stated that one angle is 100° which means that the four equal angles cannot all be 100°).

Q9 *Answer:* C

Explanation: There are two unknowns in both statements so alone they not sufficient. However, together the two statements provide a solution through a simultaneous equation.

Q10 *Answer:* Cannot tell

Explanation: If the shapes were triangles then the answer would be true but as we do not know this, before we can conclude that the shapes are similar we need to demonstrate that the angles are equal to the corresponding angles in each shape.

Practice start 7

Q1 *Answer:* E

Explanation: We cannot establish the length of the diameter with either statement. To review the properties of a circle, Google 'area of a circle' and 'radius of a circle'. To review any element of geometry, Google the quality to find the formula and relationships.

Q2 *Answer:* False

Explanation: There are 10 numbers between 1 and 50 that end in either a 2 or 8 and as a percentage of 50 this is 20% not 10%.

Q3 *Answer:* TT

Explanation: There are many quadrilaterals which have two pairs of parallel lines and interior angles that add up to 360°.

A square is one, but it is also true of a rectangle and rhombus, for example.

Q4 *Answer:* Cannot confirm

Explanation: We do not know how many women made up the whole sample of graduates who start up their own business so we cannot confirm from the information given that 1,500 women did not start up in business. For example, if the sample of 10,000 included only 1,765 women then it could be true that 1,500 (85%) did not start up in business.

Q5 *Answer:* E

Explanation: Congruent means identical so the angles of two congruent shapes would be identical, but this would also be true of similar shapes which are not identical. Statement 1 therefore cannot prove or disprove the question. Statement 2 will not prove or disprove the question either because it is possible for two shapes to have the same sizes but not be identical.

Q6 *Answer:* False

Explanation: $x + (x + 1) + (x + 2) = 57$, so $3x = 3 = 57$, $57 \div 3 = 18$, so the first number is 18 and 18 has 6 factors: 1, 2, 3, 6, 9, 18.

Q7 *Answer:* A

Explanation: Statement 1 alone is sufficient because at each vertex of a polygon the sum of the interior and exterior angles $= 360°$. So to find the number of sides divide the total sum of the interior and exterior angles by 360°. The sum of the exterior angles of any regular polygon $= 360°$, so statement 2 does not help answer the question.

Q8 *Answer:* True

Explanation: The probability of the first event is 4/52 but the probability of the second event is 3/51 (note the card, a queen, is not replaced) so the probability of the two events $= 4/52 \times 3/51 = 1/221$.

Q9 *Answer:* D

Explanation: The surface area of a cone is found with the formula $\pi r L + \pi r^2$. If we know the radius and length then the calculation can be made. In the case of statement 2 the length can be found from the height and radius.

Q10 *Answer:* False

Explanation: There are 70 − 50 + 1 numbers in the range (if you miss out the 1 then you do not count the number 50) = 21. Find the average to find the sum 50 + 70 = 120 ÷ 2 = 60 × 21 = 1,260. The correct answer is 1,260 not 1,200 (which is the answer if you counted 20 numbers not 21 in the range).

Data interpretation

Q1 *Answer:* A, Decrease

Explanation: % increase in September – October's salaries = (1200 – 1000)/1000 = 0.20 = 20%. Since August – September's increase was 25%, September – October's percentage increase has decreased in comparison (ie 25% to 20%).

Q2 *Answer:* C, $330

Explanation: Salaries total of $6,600.

Therefore, NI = 6,600 × (0.05) = $330.

Q3 *Answer:* B, 4%

Explanation: It is stated in the data set that in 2003 each outlet was located in a residential area with an average population of 135,000 and that each outlet had 5,400 customers a day. The answer is found by expressing 5,400 as a percentage of 135,000; find this by first establishing 1% of 135,000 = 1,350 and then divide 5,400 by 1,350 = 4%.

Q4 *Answer:* A, An across the board cut of 2.5% in the price of all products

Explanation: A price reduction of 2.5% would still leave Mare's prices at almost 10% above those typically charged by the competitor and so do very little if anything to assist Mare's management team in meeting the threat. Offering a series of 'added value' services not offered by the competitor such as free home delivery, longer store opening hours and online shopping would improve the customers' perception of Mare in terms of the value for money offered (Mare's customers quoted value for money as the most important factor in deciding where they shop).

Q5 *Answer:* D, $940,000

Explanation: Find the amount of profit on each of the years and the answer to the question is the difference between them. The value of sales in 2003 was $29.5m and in 2008 $34.2m and over the period Mare has shown an average 20% profit margin on the value of these sales. 29.5m × 20% = 29.5m × 0.2 = 5.9m, 34.2 × 0.2 = 6.84. The difference is 0.94m or $940,000.

Q6 *Answer:* B and C

Explanation: Maintaining a small premium in prices over the competitor (suggested answer A) will still involve a cut in prices and so still risks the impression that quality has been cut too. Only cutting the price of items that the competitor does not sell will still leave the impression that the quality has been cut on those items. Both suggested answers B and C provide the customer with some form of assurance that quality is unaffected by a price cut.

Q7 *Answer:* C, 2.394m

Explanation: The forecast was 10% less than 2008 = 34.2m × 90% = 34.2 × 0.9 = 30.78m, the actual for 2009 was 3% below 2008 = 34.2 × 97% = 33.174. The difference is 2.394m.

Q8 *Answer:* B, 60%

Explanation: Total receipts for 2007 = 9 billion, so find 5.4 as a % of 9; 9 =100%, 1% = 100 ÷ 9 = 11.11 × 5.4 = 59.99 = 60%.

Q9 *Answer:* D, 6%

Explanation: Total receipts = 4.24 + 3.76 = 8, difference between banking and finance and all other sectors = 4.24 − 3.76 = 0.48, you must find 0.48 as a % of 8. 1% = 8 ÷ 100 = 0.08, 0.48 ÷ 0.08 = 6.

Q10 *Answer:* B, 0.5%

Explanation: For 08/09 1% = 3.6 ÷ 100 = 0.036, difference = 3.654 − 3.6 = 0.054, so increase is 1.5%. for 08/09 1% =

$0.365 \div 100 = 0.0365$, difference $= 0.036$ which is close to 1% so the best estimate of the difference in % increase between the periods is 0.5%.

Q11 *Answer:* C, 65%

Explanation: $91.20 \times 85\% = 77.52$ per unit (at discount price) $\times 80$ units $= 6,201.6$ income $- 2,170.56$ cost $= 4031.04$ profit. Percentage profit $=$ profit as a % of income. Round figures to convenient sums to speed calculation, find 4030 as a % of 6200, 10% of 6200 $= 620$, $4030 \div 620 = 6.5 \times 10$ (to get 100%) $= 65\%$ profit.

Q12 *Answer:* B, 10

Explanation: $1,200 - 800 = US\$400$, and this would buy 10 ounces of silver.

Q13 *Answer:* D, 3

Explanation: $40 \times 25 = 1,000$, $3,400 - 1,000 = 2,400 \div 800 = 3$.

Q14 *Answer:* C, 30:1

Explanation: Express $13.50:0.45 as a ratio in its simplest form. Covert all sums to cents to get 1350:45; divide both sides by 45 to get the ratio 30:1.

Q15 *Answer:* B, False

Explanation: France was ranked 20th $- 3 = 17$.

Q16 *Answer:* B, False

Explanation: In 2011 Mexico was ranked 6th and Canada 4th.

Q17 *Answer:* C, Cannot tell

Explanation: Insufficient information is provided to tell if Singapore has returned to the top of the index.

Q18 *Answer:* B, South

Explanation: The price/earnings ratio of South is 7.2:0.45, which reduces to 16:1. An investor would have to pay 16 times the last reported earnings for that share; all the others represent better value.

Q19 *Answer:* A, 25:1

Explanation: Express $30:1.2 as a ratio in its simplest form. Divide both sides by 1.2 to get 25:1.

Q20 *Answer:* A, Y2, months 8 and 9

Explanation: This question calls for judgement and does not offer you the choice of saying there is insufficient information. You will also find the answer much faster if you look at the suggested answers rather than analyse the full data set. From the passage it can be inferred that the market would interpret a score over 50 more favourable than a score under 50. From this we can infer that answers B and D would not be interpreted most favourably because they begin in the 40s not the 50s. You are also told that the more over 52 the stronger the expansion. For example should the index rise from 52 to 55 in a single month this would be interpreted very favourably by the markets. From this we can infer that the most favourable period would be A, Y2, months 8 and 9 where the index moves 3 points in a single month and the increase is sustained. C, Y3 months 3 and 4 can be rejected because while it is a 2-point move to the highest in the continuous period it is followed by a sharp adjustment to contraction.

Q21 *Answer:* B, 1.8

Explanation: The mode is 45 (the value that occurs most frequently) the mean is $234 \div 5 = 46.8 = 1.8$ greater.

Q22 *Answer:* D, 45–52

Explanation: The intequartile range includes only the middle two quartiles of the range. It is used to avoid the distortions of exceptional values that will be found in the lower or upper quartiles. In the data set the range is 41–56, which gives a range of $15 + 1 = 16$ values; divide this distribution into 4 equal parts $= 4$ values and the middle 8 values 45–52 are the interquartile range.

Q23 *Answer:* D, +0.53

Explanation: The one-month figure is not the mean; to find the mean divide the year figure by 12: $6.36 \div 12 = 0.53$.

Q24 *Answer:* A, Month 6

Explanation: Gross profit $=$ Sales $-$ Cost of sales. Month 2 $= 20,000 - 13,600 = \$6,400$; Month 4 $= 40,000 - 27,200 = \$12,800$; Month 6 $= 50,000 - 33,900 = \$16,100$.

Q25 *Answer:* B, Month 2

Explanation: Operating costs = administration costs + other expenditure. Month 1 = $38,300; Month 2 = $60,900; Month 3 = $52,300; Month 4 = $45,600; Month 5 = $44,900; Month 6 = $47,800.

Q26 *Answer:* C, 28%

Explanation: 225 – sales of item 1 and 2 = 63 units of the third items sold; find 63 as a percentage of the total 225. 1% = 2.25, 63 ÷ 2.25 = 28.

Q27 *Answer:* D, Cannot tell

Explanation: The figures for 2003 and 2005 are not provided, so a total for the period cannot be established.

Q28 *Answer:* C, $117,000

Explanation: The value of sales for market A in 2006 was 115 and 119 in 2008; find the mean by adding these two values and dividing by 2.

Q29 *Answer:* False

Explanation: A niche market is a portion of the whole at which a product is aimed. It is not necessarily the most lucrative part of the market. The statement therefore is false because it is based on a false definition.

Q30 *Answer:* A, Lower the price

Explanation: One of the market research findings regarding market B is that customers perceive higher price to imply higher quality so we can infer that by lowering the price we risk undermining the customer perception of quality and this would not help sales.

Q31 *Answer:* C, 20.7

Explanation: Sales in 2006 were 18 and the figures for 2006 were 15% better and 18 × 1.15 = 20.7.

Q32 *Answer:* B, Mass advertising promoting the quality of the product

Explanation: Suggested answer A is not a break with the past because a push strategy in marketing relies on 'pushing' the product onto the market, usually with sales reps. For this reason C should also be rejected because advertising in the trade press again seeks to 'push' the product onto the shelves before the customers. Answers B and D are different, and 'pull' strategies, because they go directly to the customer who, it is hoped, seeks out the product and so help 'pull' it into the stores through popular demand. However, suggested answer D will not maintain the price premium so answer B is prefered.

Q33 *Answer:* A, 102

Explanation: The ratio of the value of sales 2003 was 120:20 which reduces to 6:1; if we divide 119 by the same ratio we get 102:17 (divide 119 by 7 = 17 × 6 = 102).

Q34 *Answer:* B, 7

Explanation: Sales in markets A and B combined in 2004 were 121 + 19 = 140; sales in 2006 in both markets were 115 + 18 = 133. 140 − 133 = 7.

Q35 *Answer:* A, 2,800

Explanation: 140 = 5%; to find 100% divide 140 by 5 = 28 and multiply by 100 = 2,800.

Q36 *Answer:* C, $3,000

Explanation: Find 0.57 as a percentage of $3.80 and multiply $20,000 by that percentage. 3.80 = 100%, 1% = 3.80 ÷ 100 = 0.038, 0.57 ÷ by 0.038 = 15, so the profit = 15%, 20,000 (the value of sales that year) × 15% = $3,000.

Q37 *Answer:* C, 1.05m

Explanation: Find the difference between 70% of 2.7m and 70% of 1.2m; 2.7m × 70% = 1.89m − 1.2 × 70% = 0.84m, 1.89 − 0.84 = 1.05m more sets sold into the EU and US territories in 2007 than 2009.

Q38 *Answer:* A, 241.5m

Explanation: The figures state than 50 sets cost £5,750 so 1 set costs £115, the total 2.1m sets sold in 2008 would therefore cost 2.1m × £115 = £241.5m.

Q39 *Answer:* A, £115

Explanation: 5,750 ÷ 50 = 115.

Q40 *Answer:* B, £45

Explanation: 1,500 + 750 = 2,250 ÷ 50 = 45.

Q41 *Answer:* D, 12%

Explanation: 128.8 − 115 = 13.8; 13.8 ÷ 115 = 0.12 × 100 = 12.

Q42 *Answer:* C, Increase by 210

Explanation: The total profit on 50 sets produced at absorption price and sold at the recommended selling price = $128.8 \times 50 - 5{,}750 = 690$, cost of 50 at absorption cost and 50 more at marginal cost = $5{,}750 + 2{,}250 = 8{,}000$, income of 100 sets sold at 89 = 8,900, profit on 50 absorption and 50 marginal sets sold at 89 = 900, profit increased by $900 - 690 = 210$.

Q43 *Answer:* A, 14%

Explanation: Cost is £8,000, profit = $91.20 \times 100 - 8{,}000 = 1{,}120$; % profit = $1{,}120 \div 8{,}000 = 0.14 \times 100 = 14$.

Q44 *Answer:* B, 13/21

Explanation: First find the average number of hours; do this by calculating the total viewing hours and ÷ by the total number of viewers. Take the midpoint in each range: viewing hours = $22 \times 300 = 4{,}400$, $27 \times 600 = 16{,}200$, $32 \times 900 = 28{,}800$, $37 \times 400 = 14{,}800$, = $64{,}200 \div$ total viewers 2,100 = 30.57 hours average. $900 + 400$ watch an average number of hours or more expressed as a fraction this = 1300/2100 or 13/21.

Q45 *Answer:* D, Sales in market B would decrease but market A would increase

Explanation: It is stated that customers in market B perceive the higher price of Morning Tea to imply higher quality; to lower the price therefore risks losing the perception of higher quality and the loss of sales. It is stated that the buy decision in market A is almost entirely down to price and that the product is sold at a modest premium over competitor brands; it is reasonable to infer therefore that to remove the premium would result in an increase in sales.

Q46 *Answer:* C, 6.3

Explanation: No year is stated in the question and the magnitude of the difference between the markets varies each year so the best answer is a mean difference over the years. Find this by totalling the values and dividing by the number of years: 479 (market A) ÷ 76 (market B) = C × 6.3, the nearest suggested answer.

Q47 *Answer:* B, Competitor brands are winning Morning Tea's market share in market A

Explanation: The figures for sales in market A do not support the suggestion that competitor brands are winning Morning Tea's market share and for this reason you should identify suggested answer B.

Q48 *Answer:* C, 4 cents

Explanation: In 2006 82,400 units were sold for a total value of $121,304.0 = $1.46 a unit. In 2005 80,000 units were sold for a total value of $120,000 = $1.5 a unit. The difference is 4 cents.

Q49 *Answer:* A, $110,274.45

Explanation: The unit value in 2004 = $1.5 (2005 value) × 97% = $1.455, units sold in 2004 = 58,300 × 1.455 = value of $84,826.5 (add value of market B + 30%) × 130% = $110,274.45.

Q50 *Answer:* D, $10,000

Explanation: Director's loans + Other loans = Total income (in Jan). Therefore, 90,000 – 80,000 = $10,000.

Q51 *Answer:* C, Right

Explanation: The price/earnings ratio is 8.8:2.2 which equates to 4:1 so an investor would have to pay only 4 times the last reported earnings for this share; all the others represent less good value.

Q52 *Answer:* A, B and C

Explanation: Only the quantity of potatoes consumed in 2011 (ie current quantities, z) is not needed. This is because the base-weighted price index is calculated as follows: $\sum pnq0/\sum p0q0$. A – w is needed to calculate p0 (ie base-year price). B – x is needed to calculate q0 (ie base-year quantity). C – y is needed to calculate pn (ie current price).

Chapter 4. Verbal assessments

Transformers and language

Q1 *Answer:* C

Explanation: The code reads may, oil, enlarge high. The best fit will use the words may and oil and a term that is an enlargement of high (eg far above the ground, soaring, sky-scraping) and it will not include any other words from the list of codes. A can be rejected because it does not include the word may, B can be rejected because it includes the word gasoline but the code for it does not occur in the question. D can be rejected because it does not include a term that is an enlarge-ment of high.

Q2 *Answer:* A

Explanation: The code reads equivalent contradiction, invest-ment, fuel, green. B is a poor fit because the code for bio is not in the question. C and D are also poor fits because they do not include equivalents to contradiction.

Q3 *Answer:* C

Explanation: The code reads enlarge new turn around know. Enlarge new and you get, for example, innovative, novel fresh, turn around know and you get, for example, unaware and guess. Suggested answer A is not a good fit because it uses the word new, B is a poor fit because it includes the word can but its code is not in the question. You can reject D because it includes could but its code is not given nor does it include a word that turns around know nor enlarges new.

Q4 *Answer:* B

Explanation: The code reads turn around green, octane, high, fuel. Turn around green can mean, for example experienced, polluting, not green. Suggested answer A fails to turnaround green, C includes more but not its code and D includes few and not its code.

Q5 *Answer:* D

Explanation: The code reads ethanol, diesel, know, decrease few. A does not fit because the word know is not used. B does not fit the code because it uses the word few rather than a decrease of few, C does not fit because minority is not a decrease of few.

Q6 *Answer:* A

Explanation: The code reads fuel, investment, turn around alternative. Suggestion B is a poor fit because its uses the term invest not investment. C can be rejected because unconventional is the same as alternative; D is a bad fit because it uses the word alternative and not its opposite.

Q7   *Answer:* A and B

Explanation: The code reads equivalent could, alcohol, green, tell; equivalents to could are might and possibly will. C is less than a perfect fit because it does not make use of an equivalent to could; D is less than best because it does not make use of the word tell.

Q8   *Answer:* D

Explanation: The code reads enlarge tell, oil, vegetable, diesel. Suggested answer A is less than a perfect fit because it uses the term alternative which is in the list of codes but not in the question code, B does not use an enlarged version of tell and C uses the term say which is not an enlarged version of tell (such as broadcast or televise) but an equivalent.

Q9   *Answer:* C

Explanation: The code reads high, few, know, may. Answer A is a less than good fit because the word know is not utilized; B is also less than perfect because the words gain and more occur in the list of codes but the codes are not present in the question. D can be rejected because it does not include the word use.

Q10 *Answer:* C

Explanation: The code reads turn around contradiction, decrease new, gain. Answer A is less than a good fit because it does not include a word that turns around contribution such as agreement, harmony or conformity. B fails because it includes the word fuel, the code for which is not included in the question. D fails because it includes the word but not the code for could and does not have a term that can be described in terms of a decrease of new (like recent, modern, up to date).

Modifiers and lexis

Q11 *Answer:* A

Explanation: The code reads append milk, parallel temperate. Append means add and bottled milk, custard, strawberry milkshake and fruit yogurt are all correct as things added or appended to milk. Parallels of temperate are pleasant or mild. A is correct because it correctly applies both codes, B, C and D can be rejected because they do not use a parallel of temperate.

Q12 *Answer:* C

Explanation: The best fit is code C which reads literally lessen tiny, pasta, plural piece, reverse popular. This can be correctly translated to read miniscule (lessen tiny) pasta pieces (plural piece) unpopular (plural piece). A is wrong because it includes the unused codes for deflation and mobile phone contracts, B is wrong because the code for cigarettes is not utilized and D is a less good fit because piece is left singular.

Q13 *Answer:* C

Explanation: The code reads parallel delete, cigarettes popular. A parallel of delete is kill or ban. A can be rejected because deadly is an expanded parallel of delete, B does not have a parallel of delete. D does not include popular.

Q14 *Answer:* B

Explanation: The code reads milk, reverse refrigerator. The only reverse of refrigerator in the suggested answers is microwave oven. Heat or cook are not the reverse of refrigerator but of refrigerate.

Q15 *Answer:* C

Explanation: The code reads plural parallel piece. A can be rejected because bit is not plural, B can be rejected because the code for wide-screen TV is not included in the code and C includes the word tiny but its code does not occur in the question.

Q16 *Answer:* D

Explanation: The code reads popular lessen soft furnishings; of the suggested answers you need to choose between B and D. You can reject A and C because table and beach towels are not soft furnishings. It's a hard call but D is preferred because it is plural so is a better translation of lesson soft furnishings than singular sofa.

Q17 *Answer:* A

Explanation: The code reads reverse add, append landscape gardening. Reverse add is to remove, minus or take away but not red. Institute of landscape gardening and landscape gardening company are valid expansions of the term landscape gardening (append) but landscape or landscape gardener are not.

Q18 *Answer:* B

Explanation: The code reads parallel service, parallel elevated. A can be rejected because a parallel of elevated is not included, C uses service not a parallel of service, D lacks a parallel of service.

Q19 *Answer:* A and B

Explanation: The code reads lessen mobile phone contracts, parallel commodity, akin unfashionable. D can be rejected because an akin of unfashionable is not used, D can also be rejected because a lessened term of mobile phone contract is not used.

Q20 *Answer:* D

Explanation: The code reads parallel gasoline, reverse deflation, akin lessen banking, against. A parallel of gasoline is aviation fuel, an akin lessened term to banking is insure (insurance is an industry akin to banking and insure is lessened). You can reject A because it does not utilize the full code, B can be rejected because banking has been lessened but an akin term is not used, C is wrong because deflation has not been reversed.

Modifiers and vocabulary

Q21 *Answer:* D

Explanation: The code reads past looks, online he or she, past looks is looked, viewed and arguably surfed the site. Suggested answers A, B and C all contain items from the list of codes not included in the question, which makes D the best fit.

Q22 *Answer:* B and C

Explanation: The code reads similar to staff, steal, reverse high. Similar to staff can mean employees, gang, team, workers and the reverse of high includes low, short and squat. Answer A includes the term try but its code is not in the question; answer D does not include the term steal.

Q23 *Answer:* A

Explanation: The code reads believe, if, ready, contract believe. Answer B is a poor fit because the word if does not occur, C does not include the word believe and D fails to make use of the term ready.

Q24 *Answer:* B

Explanation: The code reads similar to no, seems only. Suggestion A is less than the best fit because it states seem and not seems, C does not make use of the term only and D does not include a term similar to no (affirmative is the opposite of no).

Q25 *Answer:* B

Explanation: The correct code reads similar to works, he, information, similar to works. The first similar to works gives job, the second work, expand steal gives steals.

Q26 *Answer:* C

Explanation: The code reads reverse prefers, week if. Suggestion A is less than good because the term if is not used, B is at fault because it does not include the reverse of prefers and D can be rejected because the term week is not utilized.

Q27 *Answer:* D

Explanation: The code reads past believe, contract all. Suggested answer A is not perfect because it includes the word he but the code is not found in the question. Answer B is not a good fit because suppose is not in the past tense. Answer C is problematic because everyone is not a contraction of all.

Q28 *Answer:* A

Explanation: The code reads expand high, he or she, seems, Expand high can be for example gigantic, massive vast, mammoth. Answers B and C lack a word that is an expansion of high; D does not include either he or she.

Q29 *Answer:* B and C

Explanation: The code reads works, similar to no. A is a poor fit because it includes the word if but the code is not in the question. D can be rejected because unknown in the context of the sentence means anonymous, which is not similar to no.

Q30 *Answer:* B

Explanation: The code reads reverse we, he or she. The reverse of we is for example me, I myself, single-handed, alone. D fails to fit the code because it does not include either he or she. A and C fail because they use the word he and not its reverse.

Converters and key terms

Q31 *Answer:* C and D

Explanation: The code reads equivalent report, decrease better. Answer A fails to include a word that is a decrease of better (for example satisfactory, good enough, adequate, okay). B is a poor fit because it includes the word report rather than an equivalent.

Q32 *Answer:* A

Explanation: The code reads rich, decrease dishonest, must. Decrease dishonest is, for example, questionable and wrong but not cheated. Answer B is a poor fit because it does not include must; neither C nor D include a decrease on dishonest.

Q33 *Answer:* C

Explanation: The code reads industry, children, turn around accept. To turn around accept gives, for example, refuse, rebuff, discard, eliminate. Answer A does not use a term that turns around accept, answer B includes the term education but the code is not found in the question. D does not include the word children.

Q34 *Answer:* B and D

Explanation: The code reads similar public, equivalent critical. Words similar to public include community, open, civic and words equivalent to critical include decisive, key and important. Answer A lacks a word similar to public and C has no equivalent to critical.

Q35 *Answer:* A

Explanation: The code reads doubtful, equivalent merit. Words that are the equivalent of merit include value, worth and advantage. Answer B almost fits but good point is not strictly an equivalent to merit, C does not include the word doubtful only doubted, and D includes the word report which is included in the list of codes but not found in the question.

Q36 *Answer:* A

Explanation: The code reads turn around rich, decrease must, crucial. To turn around rich gives poor, not so well off; to decrease must gives should and advised. Suggested answers B and D do not include a decrease of must. C includes the word must, not a decrease of it.

Q37 *Answer:* D

Explanation: Suggested answer A reads equivalent dishonest, equivalent industry. Equivalents to dishonest are lying, false, insincere and corrupt; equivalents to industry include manufacturing, business and commerce.

Q38 *Answer:* B

Explanation: The code reads reform, public, crucial. If we add 81 which equals equivalent then we can make decisive fit because it is an equivalent of crucial.

Q39 *Answer:* B

Explanation: The code reads enlarge rich, decrease rich. To enlarge rich gives wealthy, affluent prosperous and to decrease rich gives deprived, underprivileged, needy and hard-up. A is a poor fit because it use the term children but does not include its code, C can be rejected also because it includes the term better but not its code. D is less than a good fit because it does not include a term that is the decrease of rich.

Q40 *Answer:* B and D

Explanation: The code reads education, children, and equivalent merit. Answer A can be rejected because right is not an equivalent to merit, C can be rejected because it includes the term exceed but its code is not given.

Modifiers and terms

Q41 *Answer:* B

Explanation: The code reads similar to buy, Smith. Suggested answer A can be rejected because it uses the word twenty but the question does not include the code. C and D can be rejected because sell is not similar to buy.

Q42 *Answer:* B

Explanation: The code reads expand small and similar to unique. Words that are expansions of small are big, immense and gigantic. Terms similar to unique are exclusive, rare, the only one of its kind. A and D fail because tiny and petite are not expansions of small, C can be rejected because it uses the term makes, the code for which is not provided.

Q43 *Answer:* D

Explanation: The code reads collectors, expand million. Suggested answer A uses the term bid but the question does not include the code for it, B fails because million is not expanded, and C makes use of the term stamps when the code is not provided in the question.

Q44 *Answer:* D

Explanation: The code reads similar to feature, similar to bid. Terms that are similar to feature include mark, trait and attribute; words similar to bid include offer, tender, submit and proposal. Suggested answer A can be rejected because it includes the term makes when the question does not include its code. B fails because it does not include a term similar to feature. C fails because submit is not similar to feature.

Q45 *Answer:* A and D

Explanation: the code reads price, similar to minus. Words that are similar to minus include fewer and less. Suggested answer B is less than a good fit because it includes the word sold but the code is not found in the question. Suggestion C can be rejected because it does not include the word price.

Q46 *Answer:* C

Explanation: The code reads cheap, any, price. For the sentence to fit the code, makes is required, which is 222.

Q47 *Answer:* D

Explanation: The code reads sold, reverse under, million. The reverse of under is over. Suggested answers A and C can be rejected because more and in excess are not the reverse of over; B does not fit because below is not the reverse of under.

Q48 *Answer:* A

Explanation: A makes the best fit because 100 222 reduces makes to make and 99 236 expands investment to give investments.

Q49 *Answer:* B and C

Explanation: The code reads collectors, buy, stamps, investments. Suggested answer A can be rejected because it does not make use of the word buy, suggested answer D can be rejected because it includes the word any when the code is not given.

Q50 *Answer:* D

Explanation: The code reads expand twenty, reduce twenty. Twenty can be expanded to any number or reduced to a lesser number or a term such a few. Suggested answer A can be rejected because it contains the word twenty not an expansion or reduction of it. B is less than a good fit because it includes the word sold but the code for this term is not found in the question. C can be rejected because the code for million is not given.

Verbal reasoning

Q1 *Answer:* True

Explanation: This is obviously true according to the passage where it is stated 'Sound is a mechanical wave and animals perceive sound mechanically. The senses of smell, taste and vision all involve chemical reactions, but the hearing system is based on physical movement.'

Q2 *Answer:* False

Explanation: Range could mean both frequency and amplitude but the question asks how the author uses the term and the author distinguished between them when he wrote 'To be heard these [sound] waves must be within range and sufficiently strong.' This suggests that by range the author is primarily concerned with frequency. This is supported later in the passage when normal human range is described.

Q3 *Answer:* False

Explanation: These frequencies are given as those used by whales, which you might conclude are all infrasound. However, the passage states 'Cetaceans communicate and hunt using infrasound (they also produce sound audible to humans).'

Q4 *Answer:* Cannot tell

Explanation: The fact that sound travels through air and water is discussed but the question of sound and solids is not resolved in the passage with sufficient certaity. We are told that the sense of hearing relies on physical movement, in mammals, for example, on the transfers of sound via three small bones named the hammer, anvil and stirrup to the inner ear, but transfer does not imply travelling through.

Q5 *Answer:* True

Explanation: It would be reasonable to conclude from the passage that a low-income bright child is at a considerable disadvantage. The passage states that 'A bright child from a high-income family was found to have a one in two chance of gaining a place at one of the best universities. A bright child from a low-income family had only a one in 10 chance of gaining such a place. The bright children from high-income families were themselves very likely to enjoy a high income in their working life. A significant majority of the bright children from low-income families failed to earn above the national average wage.'

Q6 *Answer:* Cannot tell

Explanation: The debate was amongst political parties and educational commentators but this does not support or disprove a conclusion that it was widespread.

Q7 *Answer:* False

Explanation: The primary finding of the research is that a divide exists between the achievements of children of similar standard.

Q8 *Answer:* Cannot tell

Explanation: Some commentators certainly argued that a child needed parental encouragement and resources such as a quiet place to study, books and internet access if they were to realize their full potential but we are not told of the report's full conclusions and we cannot infer them from the passage.

Q9 *Answer:* True

Explanation: Confounded means surprised or confused and this is a reasonable account of the colonialist attitude towards Great Zimbabwe described in the second half of the passage.

Q10 *Answer:* Cannot tell

Explanation: The passage describes the modern state as named after Great Zimbabwe but does not say that the city is located in the modern state (even though in fact it is).

Q11 *Answer:* Cannot tell

Explanation: It is reasonable to conclude that the walls are a striking feature of the ruined city but it is not possible to say from the information provided what the most striking feature is.

Q12 *Answer:* False

Explanation: The passage states that the city prospered between the 11th and 14th centuries but afterwards fell into decline and was eventually abandoned. From this it is false to infer that the city was abandoned in the 14th century.

Q13 *Answer:* False

Explanation: Cumulus clouds are described as irregularly shaped balls and so it is reasonable to describe them as lumpy. The passage describes them as knobbly, which is an acceptable alternative to lumpy. It is therefore false to say that it would be false to describe cumulus clouds as lumpy.

Q14 *Answer:* True

Explanation: The passage states 'Sunlight that hits a cloud at a shallow angle may make the cloud appear silver, yellow or even red.'

Q15 *Answer:* Cannot tell

Explanation: We are only told that from a satellite image of the clouds they will appear white, so the passage does not provide sufficient information on what we can draw from a satellite image of the clouds and we are unable to say if the statement is true.

Q16 *Answer:* True

Explanation: Fog is defined in the passage as a thick cloud of water droplets at or near ground level and it is reasonable to draw from this the statement that we can think of fog as a cloud resting on the ground.

Q17 *Answer:* False

Explanation: The word pensioner is used in the passage when it is written that in the 1960s there was one pensioner for every five workers but the passage does not state that a pensioner is a person who receives a pension.

Q18 *Answer:* True

Explanation: Purportedly means to claim to be or do something, especially to falsely claim. The fact that the author has chosen to use the term purportedly rather than, for example, supposedly does therefore imply that the claim may be false.

Q19 *Answer:* Cannot tell

Explanation: The passage states that 12 million are directly affected because they will rely on a state pension only, but we are not told how many more have an insufficient private scheme and cannot infer the information from the passage.

Q20 *Answer:* True

Explanation: The passage states that 'more than half of all working people will rely solely on the state to provide a pension in their old age' and it [the crisis facing people who will depend solely on a state pension] will directly affect around 12 million people. From this it can be inferred that 12 million equals more than half of all working people.

Q21 *Answer:* False

Explanation: The author goes on to address the issue of ice floating on water when he writes 'The crystal structure of solid water is less dense than liquid water and this is why ice floats on water' so it is not reasonable to conclude that this is also what he meant earlier in the passage.

Q22 *Answer:* Cannot tell

Explanation: The passage described a number of unique or unusual qualities of water. We can establish the first quality that is described is in fact unique because the passage states 'no other substance coexists naturally as a liquid, solid and gas on Earth's surface'. We also know that water is a uniquely powerful solvent. However, we cannot establish from the passage if the remaining qualities attributed to water are either unique or simply unusual.

Q23 *Answer:* False

Explanation: It is stated in the passage that the most distinct quality of seawater – not water – is its salinity.

Q24 *Answer:* Cannot tell

Explanation: The passage stage that most solids have higher densities than their liquid forms. No information is given about the relative densities of solid and molten iron so we cannot tell from the passage if the statement is true or false.

Q25 *Answer:* True

Explanation: The passage describes how in espionage a coded message may be written in invisible ink and encryption software programs hide encrypted files so that someone unauthorized to access the data will not even realize they are there.

Q26 *Answer:* Cannot tell

Explanation: The example of ATMs is given as one where 'to prevent fraud it is required by law that sensitive data in ATM transactions is encrypted before being transmitted between the ATM and the bank processing centre'. However, from this we cannot conclude that 'in many countries it is law that the information must be encrypted'. The example may only apply to one country or a number and not many.

Q27 *Answer:* False

Explanation: The passage states that there are a number of free encryption software programs available on the internet. So while the first part of the statement is true it is false to say that encryption is something not everyone can afford.

Q28 *Answer:* True

Explanation: The passage states that it has become imperative that data is encrypted and imperative means vitally important. The passage states that information both stored and transmitted needs to be encrypted.

Q29 *Answer:* False

Explanation: A parthenogenic birth is reproduction without fertilization. Parthenogenic is not defined in the passage and is associated with a state of chaos only in relation to the myth of Gaia.

Q30 *Answer:* Cannot tell

Explanation: The passage does not provide information on Golding's sympathy toward the Gaia theory. It is only stated that he suggested the name Gaia but this does not imply agreement.

Q31 *Answer:* False

Explanation: Lord of the Flies is described as Golding's first novel and published in 1954. The passage states that he died in 1993, which is 39 years later.

Q32 *Answer:* Cannot tell

Explanation: We are told that Lovelock's most recent book is *The Revenge of Gaia* but not which of his other titles was his first.

Q33 *Answer:* False

Explanation: The passage does not link the success of the expressive revolution to the question of whether or not audiences become adept editors. According to the passage the expressive revolution will embrace most people irrespectively, and as a consequence audiences will become adept editors.

Q34 *Answer:* False

Explanation: The passage states that the revolution is creating considerable pessimism amongst the employees of the traditional media corporations as they realize the extent to which the business model to which they have become accustomed is threatened. They can barely believe that users might put as much or more onto the network as they download. This strongly suggests that they had expected the internet to be another outlet for their products rather than a challenge to their business model.

Q35 *Answer:* False

Explanation: In the context of the passage the word expressive means conveying thoughts or opinions.

Q36 *Answer:* False

Explanation: The author provides examples to illustrate his argument when he describes 'online ratings for the restaurants they visit, sharing home-made podcasts and videologs, contributing entries to collaborative sites'. However, an analogy is a comparison between one thing and another offered as an explanation, and the author offers an analogy when he writes 'not every review or entry on the internet is correct and sure, some are bizarre. But the same has always been true of the content of our daily newspapers or favourite radio programmes.'

Q37 *Answer:* True

Explanation: The passage states that seasickness occurs when our visual reference to our surroundings and our balance organs are confused by motion. Anxiety and tiredness are described as factors that may increase the likelihood of it occurring.

Q38 *Answer:* Cannot tell

Explanation: The author does not address the subject of whether or not almost everyone will suffer seasickness: the passage states that 'some people are particularly vulnerable to seasickness while others appear immune or become immune through exposure'. But the author does not indicate how many might seem immune and if this allows for the possibility that almost everyone will get seasick.

Q39 *Answer:* False

Explanation: When the author writes 'the resulting confusion brings on nausea and vomiting', disorder would be an acceptable alternative to confusion but by complexion the author means skin colour not perspective when he writes 'their complexion is pale; they may sweat and complain of feeling clammy'.

Q40 *Answer:* True

Explanation: The question asks what could be meant by unsuitable and it is reasonable that it could mean that they are unsuitable if the individual must operate equipment, serve passengers or sail the vessel, because they cause drowsiness.

Q41 *Answer:* True

Explanation: This is a reasonable conclusion to draw from the passage where puppetry is portrayed as an ancient tradition in, for example, India and China and universal in that it is found in Asia, Africa, Europe and the New World.

Q42 *Answer:* False

Explanation: This is a question about the origins of the Chinese storyline rather than the tradition of puppetry. It's reasonable to infer that the tradition of puppetry owes its heritage to the Indus Valley, but the origins of the Chinese storyline are not described in the passage. It is possible that the Chinese tradition developed its own storylines. The European and Indonesian storylines are attributed to India but from this we cannot reasonably infer that the Chinese storyline owes its heritage to the Indian tradition. Note that had the question not started with the clause 'It is reasonable to infer' and instead stated 'The storyline in Chinese puppetry owes', then the answer would have been Cannot tell instead of False.

Q43 *Answer:* Cannot tell

Explanation: We are told that this form of art spread from India across the civilizations of Asia, Africa, Europe and even to pre-Columbus societies of Central America. We are not told how those people and puppetry got there. It might have been by sea, for example, and not a land bridge. Had the question asked if the people *may* have taken puppetry with them by land bridge then it could be debated if this would change the answer to True because may signifies a weak clause.

Q44 *Answer:* False

Explanation: The passage draws a distinction between a doll used in children's play and in public entertainment (theatre).

The author therefore may not accept the finding of a doll in a child's tomb as evidence of puppetry as theatre as it can be explained as a child's toy used in play.

Q45 *Answer:* True

Explanation: The passage states 'this name dates from a later period and is another native American people's name for cassava flour'. We are told that the Arawak people grew cassava as a staple and used it extensively in their cooking; it is true therefore that this may have been the name that another Caribbean people called the first people that Columbus met in the New World. We simply do not know given the information provided in the passage.

Q46 *Answer:* False

Explanation: It is clear that a contradiction exists because we are told that the Arawak people were 'without ferrous objects' and 'had no metals of their own and used tools and weapons expertly fashioned from stone and wood'. This raises the question of at which point the contradiction arose and whether it occurred at the description of the first meeting or somewhere else in the passage. The description of the meeting occurred in the passage before the statement that the people were without ferrous objects, so strictly speaking the contradiction arose in the passage when it is reported that the people were without ferrous objects and not at the description of the exchange of gifts at the first meeting.

Q47 *Answer:* True

Explanation: The passage states that 'his journals include very little information about the Arawaks' and we are told that 'Columbus did not say if he established what they called themselves or if he did, he did not consider it worth recording'. From this it is reasonable to infer that Columbus wrote little of the culture, customs and language of the Arawak people.

Q48 *Answer:* Cannot tell

Explanation: We are told that the Arawak populations of the Bahamas and most of the Greater and Lesser Antilles islands were annihilated but we cannot infer from the passage that their language and culture are lost. It may be for example that the records of settlers are sufficiently extensive that the language spoken by the Arawak people is preserved.

Q49 *Answer:* False

Explanation: The Scottish Parliament was re-established in 1998, 291 years after its unification with the Parliament of England to form the Parliament of Great Britain.

Q50 *Answer:* Cannot tell

Explanation: The passage states that the Scottish National Party is set to take control 11 years after the Scottish Parliament was re-established. From this we cannot tell or infer if or when they took control.

Q51 *Answer:* True

Explanation: The reality of an independent Scotland is described between the Union of Crowns and the Act of Union when it is written 'the two states remained autonomous and self-governing'; the ideal of an independent Scotland is described in relation to modern times.

Q52 *Answer:* Cannot tell

Explanation: The passage does not provide any details on the Scottish people's wishes regarding independence. The passage states that there was celebration when the devolved Scottish Parliament was re-established but this tells us nothing about the people's views on full independence.

Chapter 5. Attitudinal and personality questionnaires

Q1 There is no right or wrong answer to this question as only a team player would agree strongly with it and only an employer who prefers a team approach will be attracted to this response.

Q2 When an organization is seeking a sector specialist or an experienced manager, it is likely to be looking for someone with a full understanding of the market and competitors' trends. If you have these qualities and are seeking such a role then be sure to emphasize them.

Q3   *Answer:* 1: C, 2: C, 3: B, 4: B

Explanation: Race discrimination occurs when a person is treated less favourably on the grounds of race, colour, nationality, ethnic or national origin. It is unlawful to practise racial discrimination. Your employer is responsible for ensuring that there is no racism in the workplace. Colleagues who knowingly discriminate against another employee on the grounds of race, or who aid discriminatory practices, are also acting unlawfully. Suggested response 1 is less than acceptable because it is only concerned with the name-calling and not the other forms of discrimination described in the passage. Suggested response 2 is also less than acceptable because in the passage you are described as the only black employee so you can't talk to colleagues who might be suffering the same problems. Both 3 and 4 are acceptable responses because they might end the discrimination. Neither of the responses in isolation is the most appropriate response because it would be better if you did both and kept a record of the instances and used an official grievance procedure to give you employer the chance to put a stop to it.

Q4   Some people put their success down to these qualities and roles are advertised as ideally suited to someone who can bring determination and drive. If this applies to you and the position you are looking for then be sure to agree strongly.

Q5   Many employers put the success of their organizations down to good management and team working and they want to recruit managers who will continue these traditions.

Q6   This is a combination of skills that many employers are looking for in their managers. Consider using it as a statement on your CV and prepare a couple of examples in which you have demonstrated the ability to both think strategically and oversee the day to day, that you might refer to at interview.

Q7 *Answer:* 1: C, 2: C, 3: C, 4: A

Explanation: Whatever the size of the business, your employer has a duty of care to look after your health, safety and welfare while you are at work. This duty of care includes making sure that ventilation, temperature, lighting, and toilet, washing and rest facilities all meet health, safety and welfare requirements. This includes providing somewhere for employees to get changed and to store their own clothes and an area set aside for rest breaks and eating meals, including if necessary suitable facilities for pregnant women and nursing mothers. Response 1 is less than acceptable because you have tried before and it has failed. Response 3 is less than acceptable because it is not the case that a small business does not have a duty of care for its employees, while 3 is also less than acceptable because a tribunal would expect you to have raised the matter formally with your employer. Response 4 is the most acceptable because you have tried to resolve the issue informally and failed, and it is proper that you therefore raise the matter formally.

Q8 In the case of management, HR and sales, these skills are highly rated and for these roles many employers would only consider candidates who agreed strongly with this statement.

Q9 In creative and strategic roles these abilities are sought after. Recruiters place great value on the ability to think laterally and originally. If you are seeking such a role then be sure you can provide examples of when you demonstrated both.

Q10 I don't think many employers would be unhappy if either the margin or customer base was doubled. In the short term the doubling of margins brings much higher net profitability while doubling the customer base might bring greater long-term benefits. This statement therefore can be seen as a question of whether you take a long- or short-term view and ideally your outlook should correspond to that of your prospective employers.

Q11 *Answer:* 1: A, 2: C, 3: C, 4: B

Explanation: You should first try to resolve disagreements with co-workers informally but if this fails and despite the passing of time the matter continues, then you should involve your supervisor or manager to see if they can resolve matters. If neither of these actions works and the issue continues to affect your work, you should take the matter up formally. Do this using your employer's formal procedures for grievances. You should be able to find these in either your company's handbook or as an appendix to your contract of employment. Suggested response 1 is the most appropriate because it seeks to resolve the matter informally between the workers involved and if that fails seeks to resolve it informally with management. Responses 2 and 3 do not follow the recommended procedure so are less than acceptable while 4 is acceptable but is not the most appropriate because it does not first try to resolve things informally with your co-workers before involving management.

Q12 Some would agree but some would disagree if, for example, they consider success to be dependent on collaboration or innovation, so do your research and establish the working ethos of the company to which you have applied.

Q13 If you bring energy and determination as well as years of experience then be sure to agree with this statement.

Q14 *Answer:* 1: C, 2: A, 3: C, 4: C

Explanation: The situation states that the success of the event is yours and it is about to go wrong. Under these circumstances the only right thing to do is show leadership and go and get suitable food yourself.

Q15 *Answer:* 1: B, 2: C, 3: C, 4: B

Explanation: Your employer should have systems and procedures in place to minimize the risk of pressures that create stress. When a member of staff falls ill due to stress at work employers should review the person's role and look at ways to remove the causes of the stress and ill health. If you write to them informing them of a stress-related illness, they should respond by offering to meet you and discuss ways to help you return to work and avoid the risk of the illness reoccurring. Responses 1 and 4 would allow the employer the opportunity to meet their responsibility to adjust your workload and provide a healthy place of work and so are both acceptable. Both responses 2 and 3 and less than acceptable. Response 2 is less than acceptable because the illness was due to the amount of work and not a lack of lunch breaks or extra hours worked. Response 3 is less than acceptable because it does not seek to address your workload, which is the cause of your ill health.

Q16 Most employers would want you to agree with this statement as it implies a confident, proactive and helpful approach.

Q17 Be careful how you answer questions like this. It is investigating your attitude at work and if you indicate a response that the employer considers inappropriate it could result in your application being rejected. No employer is likely to agree that raised voices are acceptable and to raise your voice because you believe a colleague is not listening suggests you are prone to being impatient and frustrated.

Q18 *Answer:* 1: B, 2: C, 3: C, 4: A
Explanation: You can expect your boss to be able to listen to someone distressed and be able to recognize signs of stress and have some understanding of possible ill-health outcomes. It is reasonable to expect your employer to have the systems and procedures in place to minimize the risk of pressures creating stress and leading to ill health, and to be able to accommodate events such as a bereavement by making adjustments to workloads. Suggested response 1 is acceptable but more is needed before it can be described as the most appropriate. Suggested responses 2 and 3 are less than acceptable because they do not secure the change necessary for you to cope with your return to work. Suggested response 4 is the most appropriate because it is likely to reduce the pressures on you.

Q19 Some employers operate this style of working and are looking for people who would agree with this statement.

Other employers operate very differently and would prefer employees who are comfortable to work in a less regimented environment.

Q20 Obviously agree with this statement if it is true, but realize that agreement may well count against an application for many managerial positions. Things go wrong and from time to time a whole series of things go wrong and employers rely on managers who can deal with setbacks, rise to a challenge and get the job done no matter the turn of events.

Q21 In business it is not usually possible to plan for every eventuality. It is often a good idea to plan for a number of possible outcomes but a desire to plan for every possibility may risk an impression of anxiety.

Q22 In some roles and situations this approach is necessary but whether it is frequently the best approach will depend on the role to which you are applying and the working culture of the organization. Some employers encourage transparency and openness in all areas of work and may well prefer an applicant who disagrees.

Q23 *Answer:* 1: B, 2: C, 3: A, 4: C
Explanation: It would not be right under the circumstances to discuss the matter directly with your manager but it is equally not appropriate that you put up with it because it is affecting your work and upsetting you. The most appropriate responses are 1 and 3 because they will ensure that management are informed of the additional problems and so can do something about them. Suggested response 3 is the most appropriate because of the professional and empathetic approach adopted.

Q24 You might wonder what the connection is between your preferred dress code and your suitability as an applicant; on its own there is none. However, a personality questionnaire comprises many questions and a whole series of them will investigate a particular personality trait. Your response to this question along with the others will indicate your suitability for the role. For example, in some industries someone who prefers to dress quietly might be more suitable for a back-of-house role than a front-of-house position.

Q25 There is no place in work for foolishness and agreement with this statement is unlikely to support your application. We all say foolish things at home or with friends but the context of this question is work, and how you might act elsewhere is irrelevant.

Q26 Every role involves routine and after a few years every job may seem routine. For this reason be careful how you respond to statements of this sort because you do not wish to give the impression that you will become discontent with the routine aspects of the role.

Q27 *Answer:* 1: B, 2: C, 3: B, 4: B
Explanation: If there is bullying of any kind, or other behaviour that affects your health or ability to do your job then a good employer will make changes to stop it. No employer should tolerate bullying of any kind and especially not of the sort described in this situation. If the employer cannot resolve it informally then it should initiate disciplinary action against any harasser. If your employer does not take action against such an individual then you may be able to use the law to make it change its approach. Responses 1, 3 and 4 are acceptable because they support the individuals affected and should lead to a resolution. Situation 2 is less than acceptable because it is unlikely to result in a resolution.

Q28 Agreement with this is unlikely to count against you and some employers highly value agreement with it because it demonstrates commitment and responsibility.

Q29 Provided it is done in the right context and in an appropriate constructive manner most employers will prefer managers who agree with this statement.

Q30 Employers don't want grievances to endure and grudges to be harboured. Disagreements arise in work over important issues and these disagreements can become passionate because a lot can depend on the right decision. At the end of the day, however, good working relations must be quickly re-established for the good of the organization.

Q31 *Answer:* 1: C, 2: B, 3: C, 4: C

Explanation: Response 1 is less than acceptable because while it is correct that the perpetrator should be challenged it would be wrong to call someone an idiot. Responses 3 and 4 are also less than acceptable because the fact that the event happened outside work does not mean that a code of conduct does not apply or that we have to accept inappropriate banter. Response 2 is appropriate in that it will result in supporting Jane, but it is not the best possible response because it fails to challenge the behaviour of the perpetrator (which should be done in a non-confrontational way).

Q32 Remember that you are responding to these statements in the context of applying for employment and you should see every response as the opportunity to present yourself as an ideal candidate. It is unlikely that the employer is looking for someone who is most motivated by the question of the meaning of life.

Q33 Employers want staff to disclose the work-related problems they encounter. That way the problem is most likely to be resolved and not be concealed where it can become something more serious.

Q34 Some working environments are competitive, others collaborative. If you prefer a competitive workplace then seek employers who offer it and tell them of your preference. Research your perspective employer's preferred way of working to be sure it is the kind of place in which you will shine.

Q35 *Answer:* 1: C, 2: C, 3: B, 4: A

Explanation: Response 1 is less than acceptable because while you may feel that you have received enough instruction to operate the crusher it is the employer's responsibility to ensure that training and instruction are sufficient to ensure the safety of workers. Response 2 is also less than acceptable because an employer should not instruct you to operate equipment without proper instruction and training and this is irrespective of the number of employees. Response 3 is acceptable but the best response is number 4 because while you decline to operate the machinery you explain why and this gives the employer the opportunity to arrange the necessary instruction so that you can carry out your duties safely.

Q36 This is an attitudinal question and so you should be careful not to answer it in a way that implies you are dishonest. No employer will want staff who are prepared to lie. Agreeing with this statement could mean that your application is rejected.

Q37 Remember to respond to all statements in the context of work. This statement is investigating your preference for working alone or as part of a team and you should answer it in that context.

Q38 To agree with this statement would imply that you cannot always be relied on to carry out your manager's instructions and this would not be an appropriate impression.

Q39 *Answer:* 1: A, 2: C, 3: C, 4: B

Explanation: Response 1 is the best approach given that you have tried and failed to resolve the matter informally and your manager is the most appropriate person to involve next. It may well be that your manager can stop all further discussion of the subject and advise Paul that he must stop. Response 2 is unlikely to succeed so is less than acceptable because such an approach has already been tried and failed. Response 3 is less than acceptable because it does not seek to resolve the problem. You might escape the problem but you will leave your colleagues to have to deal with it. Response 4 is acceptable in that it is reasonable that you approach a personnel officer but it would be better if you first took the issue to your immediate manager and then approach personnel only if he or she is unable to resolve the matter.

Q40 Your response to this statement indicates whether or not you prefer a straightforward, matter-of-fact working situation or a more political working environment where agendas and allegiances are hidden.

Q41 Interruptions to work are an unavoidable and everyday occurrence. We may not enjoy them but we should be able to switch between tasks efficiently and they should not mean that our work suffers.

Q42 Accountability is a quality employers expect of managers and to agree with this statement risks the impression that you avoid accountability.

Q43 *Answer:* 1: C, 2: C, 3: A, 4: C
Explanation: Personal issues including family problems and emotional difficulties do sometimes impact on your work. Try as you might to keep your private life separate from your work life, inevitably when the personal issues are as great as those described in the passage then one often runs into the other. In these circumstances you have no practical alternative but to inform your manager of the difficulties and request that they accommodate your situation wherever practical. Responses 1, 2 and 4 are all less than acceptable because they do not acknowledge the fact that your personal problems are impacting on your working life. Response 3 is the most appropriate because it acknowledges the impact of your personal problems on your work and seeks to deal with it.

Q44 This is another attitudinal question. If there are some sorts of people you know you are not going to get on with then you risk the impression that you have prejudices. At work we should treat all clients and colleagues with the same respect and professionalism irrespective of what sort of person they are. Agreeing with this statement could see your application rejected.

Q45 Happy-go-lucky implies an approach of leaving things to chance and not worrying too much if they go other than expected. This kind of approach might be fine in your private life but not in your working life.

Q46 What you prefer to do in your spare time is not the context of these statements so take care you are not misled by statements of this sort. The context is whether or not you have the personality to fit the organization to which you have applied.

How you respond to each statement is an opportunity to present yourself as the ideal candidate. If the role best suits someone with an outgoing, social disposition and you have one but also enjoy reading a good book then be sure to pass over your love of reading to stress your outgoing temperament.

Q47 *Answer:* 1: C, 2: B, 3: B, 4: C

Explanation: Suggested response 1 is less than acceptable because it will mean that the individual is left unaccompanied in the building. Responses 2 and 3 are acceptable responses (neither can be identified as the most appropriate response) as any potential breach in security will be addressed. Suggested response 4 is less than acceptable because it will mean that a potential breach of security has been ignored.

Q48 To agree with the statement would be to suggest that you are not a very well organized person and this may not support your application.

Q49 Many organizations adopt a policy of transparency and openness and if you are applying for a position with such an organization then they are likely to prefer a candidate who agrees with this statement.

Q50 *Answer:* 1: C, 2: C, 3: C, 4: A

Explanation: Suggested response 1 is less than acceptable because it involves you disclosing personal details of your staff to a colleague. Response 2 is less than acceptable because a team meeting is not a suitable event in which to discuss with an individual an issue such as body odour. Response 3 is less than acceptable because the fact that someone else has also noticed the odour means that you can no longer ignore the situation. Situation 4 is the best response because it will address the issue in a confidential and appropriate manner.

Q51 This is another attitudinal question and to agree risks the impression that you do not take health and safety issues seriously enough.

Q52 Employers want managers and business leaders to have integrity and it is equally important that others know their managers and leaders have integrity so that the organizational culture is based on the principle of honesty and truthfulness.

Q53 In the context of some high-pressure sales positions or other roles where it really is 'dog eat dog' then there might be employers seeking people who would agree with this sentiment. However, for the vast majority of roles such a response is unlikely to support your application.

Q54 *Answer:* 1: C, 2: A, 3: B, 4: C

Explanation: Response 1 is less than acceptable because a threat of violence is a serious matter and should not be ignored. Response 2 is the most appropriate because it will guarantee that the matter is dealt with according to the correct procedure. Response 3 is an acceptable response because it will ensure that the matter is acted on. Response 4 is less than acceptable because it would be unreasonable to expect the person who was threatened to have to resolve the matter themselves and without the support of management.

Q55 Partisan mean to follow or be a supporter and obviously employers want managers to support the organizational objectives. However, objectivity is an essential quality in a manager because without it mistakes will happen and go unnoticed. For this reason you should perhaps answer C or D to this statement.

Q56 We might act irresponsibly at home or with our friends but not at work and so you should be able to disagree with this statement.

Q57 The way someone speaks or the speed at which they speak is no good reason to feel frustration. Should you find yourself getting frustrated it is best you do not show it.

Q58 *Answer:* 1: A, 2: C, 3: C, 4: C

Explanation: Theft is a serious matter and suggested response 1 is the most appropriate given that a theft has occurred. Suggested responses 2 and 4 are less than acceptable because they do not attribute sufficient importance to the situation and response 3 is less than acceptable because you may well not have the authority to search another member of staff's personal belongings or pockets. It would be better to leave this to the police or in-house security.

Q59 Jokes at work are an unwelcome distraction and regularly cause problems. Joking around is unacceptable at work; this is an attitudinal question and in this case to disagree could cost you your application.

Q60 *Answer:* 1: A, 2: C, 3: C, 4: B

Explanation: Most organizations have clear procedures for dealing with the press. Dealing with the journalist's request without referring to the organization's public relations procedure risks exceeding your authority, making responses 2 and 3 less than acceptable. Response 1 is the best response because as well as finding out the correct procedure it obtains the telephone number of the journalist, which means her identity can be confirmed. Response 4 would be acceptable because it will result in the correct procedure being followed.

Q61 *Answer:* 1: B, 2: C, 3: C, 4: A

Explanation: Suggested response 1 is acceptable but may risk inflaming the situation so is therefore not the most appropriate response. Suggested responses 2 and 3 are both less than acceptable because they do not prevent the person from using further bad language.

Q62 *Answer:* 1: C, 2: A, 3: C, 4: C

Explanation: If you are discontented in your role then you should draw it to the attention of your line manager as soon as is practical so that he or she has the chance to correct the situation. You should not wait until an annual review to do this or ignore how you feel while getting on with the job.

Q63 *Answer:* 1: B, 2: C, 3: C, 4: C

Explanation: Suggested responses 2 and 4, while they may seem justified under the circumstances, amount to submitting false invoices, which is a criminal offence. Response 3 is less than acceptable because it is unlikely to succeed as the passage states that the employer is strict and will not refund expenses not supported by receipts.

Q64 *Answer:* 1: A, 2: B, 3: C, 4: C

Explanation: Response 1 is the most appropriate because it prioritizes team building and will ensure the team and you get to know each other. Response 2 is acceptable but places less emphasis on team building. Responses 3 and 4 are less than acceptable because they place no emphasis on the need to build the new team.

Q65 *Answer:* 1: C, 2: C, 3: A, 4: C

Explanation: Response 1 would be less than acceptable because it would involve disclosing the personal circumstances of the individual to the team. Response 2 would be less than acceptable because you would first have to see if you can arrange things differently before you agree to the request. Response 4 is less than acceptable because treating everyone equally does not mean that you cannot accommodate differences or people's changed circumstances.

Q66 *Answer:* 1: B, 2: C, 3: A, 4: C

Explanation: Response 1 is acceptable because it clarifies the worker's role and responsibilities and invites him to come and talk more. Responses 2 and 4 are less than acceptable because they do not offer the worker the support and help a manager should offer a worker. Response 3 is the most appropriate because it invites his views on what might help and offers to reorganize things differently.

Q67 *Answer:* 1: A, 2: C, 3: C, 4: C

Explanation: Response A is the most appropriate because it offers to organize things in a way that best accommodates her differences and in this instance disabilities. Response 2 is less than appropriate because equality of opportunity does not mean that we do not make exceptions or arrange things differently to accommodate differences between us. Responses 3 and 4 are also less than acceptable because both present the disability as a problem and a matter of concern.

Q68 *Answer:* 1: C, 2: B, 3: A, 4: C

Explanation: Discriminating against an applicant on the basis of gender is a matter that would need to be undertaken with great care to ensure that it was fair (in the vast majority of situations it would not be). Responses 1 and 4 therefore are less than acceptable because they do not seek clarification or advice on such a serious matter. Response 3 is the most acceptable because it involves the advice of a specialist. Response 2 is acceptable because it involves referring to the written documents and procedure for guidance before making a decision.

Q69 *Answer:* 1: C, 2: C, 3: B, 4: A

Explanation: Responses 1 and 2 almost certainly mean that you exceed your authority and allow a precedent to become established which the human resources department would not welcome and would have wished to be informed about prior to its implementation. Response 3 is acceptable but given the history of the case is unlikely to result in a lasting improvement in timekeeping. Response 4 is the most acceptable as it follows the requirement of involving an HR specialist. The consequences of that meeting are not something that you should concern yourself with.

Q70 *Answer:* 1: C, 2: B, 3: C, 4: A

Explanation: Responses 1 and 3 would be less than acceptable because neither relies on any sort of investigation into the facts of the matter. Response 2 is acceptable because it takes the complaint seriously and involves an investigation. Response 4 is the most acceptable because it involves the most complete investigation.

Chapter 6. Non-verbal assessments

Input-type diagrammatic tests

Q1   *Answer:* D, no fault

Explanation: Rule AB requires that the last character (K) is deleted, rule FG sees the fifth character (U) replaced with the next in the alphabet which is V, GH requires that the whole sequence is reversed. So the sequence has been correctly inputted and therefore there is no fault.

Q2   *Answer:* C

Explanation: The first instruction (HI) requires the T to be deleted, EF sees the L replaced with a K, finally CD should see a P inserted between the 3rd and 4th character but it has been inserted between the 2nd and 3rd so a fault occurred at C.

Q3   *Answer:* B

Explanation: In step B all letters should have been reversed; however the first and last letters have not been. So a fault occurred at B.

Q4   *Answer:* C

Explanation: The letter D deleted at step B has returned.

Q5   *Answer:* D

Explanation: The instructions have been correctly applied so there is no fault.

Q6   *Answer:* A

Explanation: The letter 'V' has been omitted and if correct the code should read BVEFGKLQ.

Q7   *Answer:* C

Explanation: The SA at step C has been inserted between the 7th and 8th and not the 6th and 7th.

Q8   *Answer:* C

Explanation: The 2nd and 4th not 2nd and 5th characters have been exchanged at C.

Q9   *Answer:* B

Explanation: The second letter at step B should be an S not a T.

Q10 *Answer:* D

Explanation: The codes have been correctly applied so there is no fault.

Q11 *Answer:* A

Explanation: The correct sequence should read BA233KEVQ because the third letter is W.

Q12 *Answer:* C

Explanation: The second not first letter has been replaced.

Q13 *Answer:* B

Explanation: The fifth letter has been reinstated after it was replaced at set A.

Q14 *Answer:* A

Explanation: A number 2 has been incorrectly inserted; the code should read BAZ7801SP.

Q15 *Answer:* D

Explanation: The codes have been implemented without fault.

Q16 *Answer:* D

Explanation: The end product is correct so no fault occurred.

Q17 *Answer:* A

Explanation: A fault occurred at step A because the third character was not deleted.

Q18 *Answer:* C

Explanation: The third character has not been replaced with the number 5.

Q19 *Answer:* B

Explanation: The fifth character has been replaced with the letter before it in the alphabet not the letter after it.

Q20 *Answer:* D

Explanation: The codes have been applied without fault.

Q21 *Answer:* C

Explanation: The correct code should read FLCCATX; the 3rd and middle characters have been switched when the step required the middle character to be replaced with a C.

Q22 *Answer:* B

Explanation: The 2nd and 5th characters have not been switched.

Q23 *Answer:* A

Explanation: The letter C introduced at step A has been omitted.

Q24 *Answer:* D

Explanation: The set of codes has been correctly inputted so there is no fault.

Q25 *Answer:* B

Explanation: The letters AS have been inserted when the instruction was to insert the letters SA.

Q26 *Answer:* D

Explanation: The codes have been applied correctly so no fault has occurred.

Q27 *Answer:* A

Explanation: The letter O and not N was inserted at step A.

Q28 *Answer:* C

Explanation: The last character has not been deleted.

Q29 *Answer:* C

Explanation: The fourth character not the fifth has been moved to the end of the sequence.

Q30 *Answer:* B

Explanation: The fourth not third character has been deleted.

Q31 *Answer:* A

Explanation: The 3rd and 5th not 2nd and 5th characters have been switched.

Q32 *Answer:* C

Explanation: The U not the middle character (T) has been deleted.

Q33 *Answer:* A

Explanation: The last character R has not been moved at step A.

Q34 *Answer:* D

Explanation: The codes have been applied without fault.

Q35 *Answer:* C

Explanation: The first character I has not been deleted.

Q36 *Answer:* D

Explanation: The codes have been applied without fault.

Q37 *Answer:* A

Explanation: The second from last character has been deleted instead of the last.

Q38 *Answer:* B

Explanation: The first and last characters were not switched.

Q39 *Answer:* C

Explanation: The last character has not been deleted.

Q40 *Answer:* B

Explanation: The third not fifth character has been deleted.

Q41 *Answer:* C

Explanation: The first character has not been deleted.

Q42 *Answer:* D

Explanation: The steps have been implemented correctly so there is no fault.

Q43 *Answer:* D

Explanation: The steps have been implemented correctly so there is no fault.

Q44 *Answer:* B

Explanation: The last character has not been deleted.

Q45 *Answer:* C

Explanation: The sequence has not been reversed the second time.

Q46 *Answer:* D

Explanation: All steps in the process went without fault.

Q47 *Answer:* C

Explanation: An unshaded square has been omitted from the final sequence.

Q48 *Answer:* A

Explanation: The square should not be shaded.

Q49 *Answer:* A

Explanation: The shaded triangle has been placed between the 2nd and 3rd not 3rd and 4th items.

Q50 *Answer:* C

Explanation: The change for code ▼ not code ▲ has been implemented at step C.

Q51 *Answer:* C

Explanation: The change at step C was not implemented.

Q52 *Answer:* B

Explanation: The last shape has not been shaded.

Q53 *Answer:* C

Explanation: The first shape has not been replaced.

Q54 *Answer:* D

Explanation: No fault occurred in the implementation of the steps.

Q55 *Answer:* D

Explanation: No fault occurred.

Q56 *Answer:* C

Explanation: The order of shapes has not been reversed.

Q57 *Answer:* B

Explanation: The shaded triangle should have become an unshaded square.

Q58 *Answer:* D

Explanation: The steps have been implemented without fault.

Q59 *Answer:* A

Explanation: An unshaded triangle and not a shaded triangle has been inserted.

Q60 *Answer:* C

Explanation: If every other shape had been correctly deleted there would have been only two shapes remaining and they would be a shaded circle and square.

Q61 *Answer:* C

Explanation: The fifth characters have not been exchanged.

Q62 *Answer:* A

Explanation: The L has been inserted into the bottom not top sequence.

Q63 *Answer:* D

Explanation: The steps have been implemented without fault.

Q64 *Answer:* A

Explanation: The fourth characters have not been exchanged.

Q65 *Answer:* D

Explanation: The steps have been implemented without fault.

Abstract reasoning

Identify a quality in common

Q1 *Answer:* A

Explanation: A third of the items differ from the rest that make up the question shape because they are either shaded or face a different direction. Suggested answer A also has one third of the items different.

Q2 *Answer:* D

Explanation: The question shapes are made up of one large and two small shapes and none of the suggested answers shares these features.

Q3 *Answer:* B

Explanation: The total number of items making up the question shapes is divisible by 3 as is the number of items making up suggested answer B.

Q4 *Answer:* A

Explanation: The question shapes include four shaded and four unshaded shapes as does suggested answer A.

Q5 *Answer:* D

Explanation: The question shapes are made up of wavy and parallel lines, triangles and squares. One of the shapes is made up of five items, the other eight. None of the suggested answers shares these features.

Q6 *Answer:* A

Explanation: The items making up the question shapes both have a total of 12 sides. Suggested answer A is also made up of items with a total of 12 sides.

Q7 *Answer:* A

Explanation: There are a total of three and seven items respectively in the question shapes and both 3 and 7 are prime numbers and the number of items making up suggested answer A (5) is also a prime number.

Q8 *Answer:* C

Explanation: The question shapes are made up of a circle, two triangles and a square. The smallest of the four items is shaded. Suggested answer C shares these qualities.

Q9 *Answer:* D

Explanation: The number of sides to the items making up the question shapes corresponds to the number of circles (eg one square, four circles). None of the suggested answers shares this feature or any other with the question shapes.

Q10 *Answer:* B

Explanation: The question shapes are made up of two and three items; 2 and 3 are the first two prime numbers. The next prime number is 5, which is the number of items making up suggested answer B.

Complete a series

Q11 *Answer:* A

Explanation: The shading is alternating on both items as the shape rotates anticlockwise.

Q12 *Answer:* D

Explanation: The triangle changes into a square and then back to a triangle each step in the series and the direction of the arrow alternates. For there to be a correct answer the arrow would have to be pointing upwards with a triangle in the left-hand corner.

Q13 *Answer:* C

Explanation: The number of shaded circles increases while the number of crosses decreases.

Q14 *Answer:* B

Explanation: The shading of the circles is alternating between all of them to half of them; the triangles are transforming to squares and then back again.

Q15 *Answer:* A

Explanation: The shapes are being removed in an anticlockwise direction starting with the square.

Q16 *Answer:* D

Explanation: The L shape is rotating in an anticlockwise direction and the diamond changes into a square and back again. For there to be a correct answer the corner of the L would have to be in the bottom left-hand corner with a diamond.

Q17 *Answer:* C

Explanation: The number of sides of the shapes follows the sequence of square numbers: 36, 25, 16, 9, 4.

Q18 *Answer:* A

Explanation: The obscured part of the 'pie' is rotating clockwise and as it passes it changes all shapes to circles.

Q19 *Answer:* B

Explanation: The number of circles follows the sequence of the whole-number factors of 8: 1, 2, 4, 8.

Q20 *Answer:* C

Explanation: Starting with squares at each step, two are transformed into circles and relocate to the bottom of the shape. Once all the squares are transformed the sequence reverses, with two squares and two circles.

Identify the correct code

Q21 *Answer:* PS

Explanation: P refers to a partially covered circle and S to shading inside a shape. The type of shading is irrelevant.

Q22 *Answer:* VW

Explanation: V refers to large shapes and W to an un-shaded background.

Q23 *Answer:* BG

Explanation: A four-sided shape is coded B and three squares on the right coded G.

Q24 *Answer:* NK

Explanation: Adjoining circles are represented by the code K; N is the code for two circles.

Q25 *Answer:* TC

Explanation: A big square is coded with the letter C; an arrow pointing to the left (whatever its size) is coded with the letter T.

Q26 *Answer:* XCA

Explanation: A circle is coded X, a semicircle Y, shading B, no shading C, an arrow shape pointing downwards A and an arrow shape pointing upwards D.

Q27 *Answer:* AEP

Explanation: When the oblong is horizontal it is coded with the letter A, and when upright with the letter B, one diagonal line is coded E and two D, four triangles around the edge of the oblong are coded Y, three triangles Z, two triangles P and one triangle W.

Q28 *Answer:* BNX

Explanation: When the right-angled triangle is in the top right-hand corner it is coded B; when a circle in found inside the triangle it is coded M; and when there is no circle it is coded N; when the hypotenuse is a thick line it is coded X.

Q29 *Answer:* CEY

Explanation: When the overlapping circles create two segments this is coded C; when the shading forms a semicircle it is coded E; and when no square is found in the left-hand corner it is coded Y.

Q30 *Answer:* AHX

Explanation: A diamond is signified by the letter A, three wavy lines by the letter H, and when the box is divided vertically it is coded X.

Allocate the three question shapes to the correct set

Q31 *Answer:*

	A	B	N
1	X		
2		X	
3		X	

Explanation: The relationship is number of sides of the question shape to the number of items in the sets. All the items in set A total an odd number, set B an even number. Question shape 1 has an odd number of sides so belongs to set A; question shapes 2 and 3 have an even number of sides so belong to set B.

Q32 *Answer:*

	A	B	N
1			X
2		X	
3			X

Explanation: Question shape 1 comprises six items belonging to neither set; question shape 2 is made of five shapes so belongs to set B; question shape 3 could belong to set A if there were no shading because the shape is rotating and the shading is alternating.

Q33 *Answer:*

	A	B	N
1			X
2		X	
3	X		

Explanation: Shape 2 with 4 shaded shapes follow set A with 0, 1, 2, 3, 4 shaded shapes. Shape 3 has 4 items so follows set B 1, 2, 3, 4 unshaded items; shape 1 follows neither rule.

Q34 *Answer:*

	A	B	N
1	X		
2		X	
3			X

Explanation: The items in set A are increasing 1, 3, 5 and alternate circles and squares so the next in the sequence would be seven squares. In set B the shading is switching left to right and the centre shape is divided into a decreasing number of segments starting 5, 4, 3 so the next in the series would be shading to the right and the central shape divided into two segments. Shape 3 does not comply with either set.

Q35 *Answer:*

	A	B	N
1			X
2	X		
3		X	

Explanation: In set A the small circle is moving anticlockwise around the larger circle from 12 o'clock to 9 to 6 and the next step would be 3 o'clock, as shown in question shape 2. In set B the number of unshaded shapes is decreasing 10, 8, 6 and the next set in the series would be four unshaded shapes as shown in question shape 3.

Q36 *Answer:*

	A	B	N
1	X		
2		X	
3			X

Explanation: In set A the number of sides is increasing 4, 6, 8; next would be 10 as in question shape 1. In set B the number of shaded shapes is decreasing by one from 4, 3, 2; the next would be 1 as found in question shape 2.

Q37 *Answer:*

	A	B	N
1		X	
2			X
3	X		

Explanation: In set B the number of shapes is decreasing by 2 each time and the next step is shown by question shape 1. In set A the number of shapes is increasing 1, 3, 6 so next is 9, as shown in question shape 3.

Q38 *Answer:*

	A	B	N
1			X
2			X
3	X		

Explanation: In set A the number of shapes is decreasing 9, 7, 5 with a central shape that is shaded. The next step in this sequence would be three shapes, the central one shaded, as shown in question shape 3. For a question shape to belong to set B it would have to comprise either zero shapes (to precede the first in the set) or four crosses with a total of 48 sides.

Q39 *Answer:*

	A	B	N
1			X
2	X		
3		X	

Explanation: In set A the number of sides to the shapes combined is decreasing 10, 8, 6 and the shaded circles are alternating inside and outside the shapes or shape.

Question shape 2 fits with this sequence. In set B one square is transformed into a triangle each step until all become triangles, as shown in question shape 3.

Q40 *Answer:*

	A	B	N
1	X		
2			X
3		X	

Explanation: From the bottom of set A the number of circles is increasing 9, 10, 11 and next is 12, as shown in shape 1. From the top of set B the circle made of 12 circles starts with four shaded and four segments decreasing to 3/3 then 2/2; the next step of shape 3 is with one shaded circle and one line dividing the circle shape made from the smaller circles.

Spatial recognition and visual estimation

Type 1. Identify the plan of the three-dimensional shape

Q41 *Answer:* C
Explanation: A) shows the right side; B) shows the left side.

Q42 *Answer:* C
Explanation: A) shows the left side; B) shows the right side.

Q43 *Answer:* A
Explanation: In B) the middle part is too long; C) has too many edges (count them and compare with the original).

Q44 *Answer:* B
Explanation: A) shows the right side; and C) shows the left side.

Q45 *Answer:* A
Explanation: All you can see from above is the three steps; in B) this zigzag form is not part of the original; C) shows the right side.

Type *2*. Identify the shape that has been rotated but is otherwise identical to the question shape

Q46 *Answer:* B

Explanation: In A) the small 'roof' shape has been moved; in C) the small 'roof' shape is missing; in D) the central part of the shape is too small.

Q47 *Answer:* A

Explanation: B) is wrong because it represents an extruded irregular quadrangle; in C) the shape has been shortened; in D) the shape has been lengthened.

Q48 *Answer:* D

Explanation: In A), B) and C) the rectangular shape has been moved.

Q49 *Answer:* B

Explanation: It is the only one with a 'roof' on the intersection of the L shape.

Q50 *Answer:* A

Explanation: B) has a W shape instead of a T shape; C) has a Z shape instead of a T shape.

Type *3*. Identify the new shape that could be constructed if the two example shapes were combined

Q51 *Answer:* C

Explanation: In A) the triangular shape has been deformed; in B) and D) the cube has been deformed.

Q52 *Answer:* D

Explanation: In A) the big triangular shape has been thickened; in B) the big triangular shape has been thinned; in C) the small triangular shape has been deformed.

Q53 *Answer:* A

Explanation: In B) there are too many lines; in C) the right triangular shape has been truncated; in D) both triangular shapes have had the edges cut off.

Q54 *Answer:* B

Explanation: In A) and C) the small cube has been moved.

Q55 *Answer:* A

Explanation: In B) and C) the hexagonal shape has been deformed.